BEFORE YOU STEP INTO THE PULPIT

H. Maurice Lednicky

Preach the word!

Blessings!

H. Maurice Lednicky

Publishing and design assistance provided by:
Life Publishers International
1625 N Robberson Ave.
Springfield, MO 65803
U.S.A.

ISBN: 978-0-7361-0489-0
Printed In U.S.A.

TABLE OF CONTENTS

PREFACE

The greatest privilege for any Child of God is to be chosen as a "spokesperson" for the Almighty God. The Apostle Paul declared,

And I thank Christ Jesus our Lord, who hath enabled me, for that he counted me faithful, putting me into the ministry.
(1 Timothy 1:12 KJV)

I was "called" to preach at the age of nine in a small Sunday School class. The teacher, often with tears in his eyes, challenged us to listen for the voice of God who would reveal His plan. He further explained that we must always be obedient and submissive to what God had chosen for us. Like young Samuel in the Old Testament (1 Samuel 3), I was not certain all that was involved in hearing God's voice. But, I do know that I heard His voice—never has there been any question in my heart about that. My first "attempt" at preaching came at age thirteen. I spoke about eight minutes and said everything I had prepared to say—three times! Since I was eighteen years old, it has been my great joy and honor to preach the Word of God in various venues all around the world. Thank God for merciful saints who were willing to listen and encourage me to keep pressing forward in obedience to His call!

Now, I am reflecting on more than sixty years since I heard His voice in that small, unpretentious room on that Sunday morning. For more than half a century, it has been my singular desire to preach His Word. At times it was to a very small group; on other occasions it has been to extremely large crowds. The number in the audience did not matter. I was honored to do what God had called me to do.

Hopefully, the underlying message of this volume about preaching will be both challenging and encouraging. Challenging, so that you will strive to become your very best for Jesus. Never stop learning. Absorb the Word of God into your mind and heart. Encouraging, as a reminder that God will always equip you for the occasion. Allow the Holy Spirit to inspire and excite you with Holy Truth. His Word will accomplish its God-given purpose wherever He sends you.

"Rightly divide the Word of Truth..."

Hermeneutics—proper interpretation of Scripture

Homiletics—proper application of Scripture

Having a foundation (Hermeneutics) without structure (Homiletics) is incomplete.

Having a structure (Homiletics) without a foundation (Hermeneutics) is impossible.

H. MAURICE LEDNICKY

ONE

UNDERSTANDING THE "CALL" TO PULPIT MINISTRY

According to the Scriptures every believer is to be a "witness" for Christ. No Spirit filled believer is ever exempted from telling others of his/her personal encounter with Christ (Acts 1:8; Colossians 4:6; 1 Peter 3:15). However, there is a major distinction between sharing your faith in the provision of Christ on the Cross in daily life and being "called" to "lead, feed, and tend the flock of God by example" (1 Peter 5:1-4).

First, examine the Old Testament carefully and it becomes obvious that God Himself selected priests (under the Mosaic Covenant) for service/ministry in both the Tabernacle and later the Temple. Aaron was the first High Priest and the Tribe of Levi was chosen to fulfill the responsibilities as priests and perform other services related to the Tabernacle and Temple (Leviticus 8:30, chapters 21-22). These very special servants of the Lord were not only selected by the Lord Himself, but were also required to live by a different and higher standard than the other Israelites. The very fact that the Levities did not have an "inheritance of land" as did the other Twelve Tribes of Israel, and were instructed to live among all the Tribes, indicates that they were "set apart" to minister in every part of the nation.

OLD TESTAMENT PROPHETS

Likewise, the hand of the Almighty was upon the prophets who were chosen by God Himself for a special ministry to His people, Israel.

For the most part, these prophets spoke during the "Kingdom" years of Israel. That is, the time period that began with Samuel and concluded with Malachi. Specifically, this would encompass the years from the anointing of King Saul to the final King of Judah, Zedekiah, who was serving at the time of the Babylonian captivity. There was a total of 16 prophets who wrote 17 books in the Old Testament (Jeremiah wrote two books), who collectively served over a period of approximately 400 years (from 800 BC to 400 BC). Elijah and Elisha were also prophets of Godly power and significance in the nation of Israel, but they did not write Old Testament books.

Perhaps we are most familiar with the four "major" prophets—Isaiah, Jeremiah, Ezekiel, and Daniel. Each of these men was called to a distinctive time and place in the history of Israel.

Isaiah—known as the Messianic prophet, as he spoke more about the coming of Christ to earth than any other Old Testament prophet. Subsequently, Isaiah is quoted more frequently in the New Testament than any other Old Testament prophet. Isaiah, whose father was a brother of King Uzziah, was from an affluent, influential family in Jerusalem. This seems to be an exception, not because God has a bias against the wealthy, but because the wealthy are often self-reliant and do not come close enough to hear the voice of the Lord.

The record of Isaiah 6:1-11 is one of the most dramatic encounters with God—and response to the call—to be found in all of Holy Writ. There is a simple pattern in Isaiah's personal call to a prophetic ministry that has often been replicated in modern times.

Notice the progression of Divine revelation that brought the prophet to a total commitment and willingness to become the Lord's mouthpiece to the nation of Israel.

UPWARD VISION	6:1-4	"saw the Lord..."
INWARD VISION	6:5-7	"saw himself..."
OUTWARD VISION	6:8-11	"saw others..."

Jeremiah—was known as the Weeping prophet. As he saw the gross sin of Jerusalem and the inevitable judgment of God that soon would come he was overwhelmed. Quite opposite from Isaiah, Jeremiah was a "country boy" who came to the city, and there he was rejected by the socially religious leaders, who only wanted to speak of peace and prosperity. Once again, there is drama in the direct call of Jeremiah to be a spokesperson for God. God revealed His own plan for Jeremiah (1:5). But, as is often the case, Jeremiah resisted the call and told God that he was not qualified (not old enough, not trained adequately, etc.) to speak for God (1:6-7). Now God is so emphatic that He told Jeremiah that He would even put the words in his mouth (1:8-10)!

Ezekiel—prophesied mainly to the Jewish captives in Babylon. In the opening chapters (1-3) of his book, the young priest-in-training recounts his vision and the strong language by which God spoke to him. God even went so far as to say that if Ezekiel did not deliver His message to the hard hearted people of Israel, he would be held accountable by God Himself (Ezekiel 3:16-27). Remember, the people of Israel had been taken into captivity as a result of turning to false gods and worshipping idols. Repeatedly, in fact, more than sixty times, the expression "They shall know that I am the Lord..." is recorded in the messages that Ezekiel proclaimed to the Jews who were suffering the consequences of their idolatry in Babylon.

Daniel—is the Old Testament prophet who had a unique platform in the palaces of five kings. But, it should be noted that as a young Jewish man, Daniel was also taken into Babylonian captivity.

While God's plan for him was unique, we must not forget that Daniel stayed true to the One True God during great tests and persecution. Daniel's integrity before God and with men earned him the right for his voice to be heard among both Jews and Gentiles.

In the light of worldwide significance, Daniel was the clearest voice among the Old Testament prophets concerning end time events. His writings are linked very closely with the New Testament book of Revelation. To this very day, some of Daniel's prophecies which were uttered more than 2,000 years ago have not yet been fulfilled.

As an aside, each person who is "called" by God to be one of His spokesperson is given a unique and important place of service. Size of the audience, popularity, prominence, or any other feature that may be deemed as "success" by the world's definition should never produce pride or lead to discouragement for the servant of the Most High God. Family heritage, social or economic status, level of academic training, do not earn nor preclude God's call.

You, alone, can do what God has called you to do. In the measure of God's plan, no person is of greater importance than any one of His obedient servants. Be faithful to do what God has called you to do—that, and that alone, is the basis for your future eternal reward!

God's choices may not always be in sync with the views of men. From just these four prophets, it is clear that the background of each is unique. Isaiah was from an affluent, politically connected family. His father was a brother of King Uzziah. Jeremiah was from a small village about 20 kilometers outside of Jerusalem. Nothing in Scripture seems to indicate that he had any pre-prophet recognition or influence. Ezekiel was from a priestly family and was a young priest-in-training when he was taken into Babylonian captivity. Daniel was a brilliant, academically mind young man who has chosen to learn the language, culture, and arts of the Babylonians. In spite of this political opportunity, Daniel did not allow his position in the palace to replace his personal dedication to Almighty God.

A quick study of the other Old Testament prophets will reveal that very little or nothing is known about the background or families of many of these God called men. A few among them were herdsmen or farmers, with an occasional priest or descendant of a previous King of Judah. The point is that God's does not have a vetting process by which He eliminates certain individuals who do not have the credentials that would allow them a position of prestige. In His sovereign wisdom God chooses whom He will. None of us were chosen because of what we can "offer to God." Rather, in His infinite foreknowledge, the Creator and Ruler of the universe sees what we could become by obediently following His leadership.

NEW TESTAMENT DISCIPLES/APOSTLES

Jesus personally chose the Twelve to be with Him. He was their mentor, training them to preach the Good News after He ascended back into Heaven.

> *Follow Me…I will make you fishers of men.*
> (Matthew 4:19 KJV)

> *You have not chosen Me, but I have chosen you.*
> (John 15:16 KJV)

> *As the Father hath sent Me, so send I you.*
> (John 20:21 KJV)

> *Go into all the world and preach the Gospel to every creature.*
> (Mark 16:15 KJV)

> *You will receive power when the Holy Spirit comes on you. And you will be my witnesses, telling people about Me everywhere—in Jerusalem, throughout Judea, in Samaria, and to the ends of the earth.*
> (Acts 1:8 NLT)

There can be no doubt of our Lord's intention. He knew that His time on earth was limited. If this message of forgiveness, redemption and restoration was going to be heard by the people of *"Jerusalem, Judea, Samaria, and all the world"* (Acts 1:8), it would be told by those He had selected. This is one of the Bible's most prolific and straight forward commands. It was intended to break down the barriers of (1) religion, (2) culture, (3) language, (4) ethnicity and (5) political persuasion. In short, Jesus died so that everyone could be restored to right relationship with God through His sacrifice. The glorious truth of man's reconciliation with the Creator God must be the singular focus of those He has anointed to carry His message.

The dramatic conversion and "call" of Saul of Tarsus (later the Apostle Paul) leaves no room for speculation about the plan that God had for his life (Acts 9:1-22). This, now converted Jewish scholar (1) wrote almost one-half of the New Testament, declaring what the Holy Spirit had revealed to him, (2) established churches all across Asia and into Europe, (3) was in prison in Rome and ultimately was (4) put to death for his faith. There is no pride or arrogance—just contentment in knowing that in Christ he is able to withstand any trail or persecution for the sake of Christ (Philippians 4:10-13). The call was so intense that everything else lost its luster in his determination to "(uncompromisingly) *fight the good fight,* (persevere) *to finish the race, and* (be steadfastly) *faithful until death"* (2 Timothy 4:6-8) (additions mine).

Only a casual review of early Church history reveals that all of the Apostles (except John the Beloved) were put to death for their faith. Such devotion was motivated by love for the Master—Jesus had personally invested in their lives. There could be no turning back!

Going forward from New Testament times until the 21st century, Paul emphasizes that specific gifts of spiritual leadership have been given to the Church. *"Now these are the gifts that Christ gave to the church: the apostles, the prophets, the evangelists, and the pastors and teachers. Their responsibility is to equip God's people to do His work and to build up the church, the body of Christ"* (Ephesians 4:11-12, NLT). To be certain, the Apostle was not giving a list by "rank" or official position, rather by the specific ministry/service that would be provided in order for the Great Commission to be fulfilled.

The call of God is a sacred privilege. It does not mean that one preaches until problems arise or there is a better position made available. No alternate plan should be chosen, just in case the ministry does not work out as anticipated. As a young preacher I heard a well known minister say, "If you can do anything other than peach, you should do it." At first this sounded a bit strange, even unspiritual. Now, I understand that he was emphasizing the serious nature of the "call of God." Preaching is not a "profession" that you select based on your personality or aptitude. If the Eternal God has chosen you to proclaim the eternal Truth, never even consider another path or option.

> *How then shall they call on him in whom they have not believed?*
> *And how shall they believe in him of whom they have not heard?*
> *And how shall they hear without a preacher? And how shall they*
> *preach except they be sent? As it is written, How beautiful are*
> *the feet of them that preach the gospel of peace, and bring glad*
> *tidings of good things.*
> (Romans 10:14-15 KJV)

TWO

IMPORTANCE OF PREACHING IN SCRIPTURE

*T*he Greek words for preach and teach are used frequently in New Testament Scripture (Teach—approximately 100 times; Preach—approximately 130 times). These words when properly translated indicate the significance of both the content and the purpose of the message. A detailed language study seems to indicate that preaching and teaching were considered synonymous activities in New Testament record. That is, for preaching to be the most effective, there must be an obvious component of teaching included. Some scholars today interpret the ministry of the "pastor" and "teacher" (Ephesians 4:12) as one, rather than encompassing two separate ministries in the Church. To settle our minds on the relationship between preaching and teaching, it is helpful to fully dismiss the idea of style or method. For example, in the Sermon on the Mount, Jesus sat and "taught" the multitude (Matthew 5:1). Yet, He was "proclaiming" truth that surely encompassed both preaching and teaching. When you are preaching the Word, you are offering instruction/knowledge of Eternal Truth. Paul says it succinctly:

So then faith cometh by hearing, and hearing by the word of God.
(Romans 10:17 KJV)

The content is the Word of God—the purpose is to bring men to faith in Christ.

EXAMPLE/INSTRUCTION OF JESUS

And Jesus went about all the cities and villages, teaching in their synagogues, and preaching the gospel of the kingdom...
(Matthew 9:35 KJV)

When Jesus had made an end of commanding His twelve disciples,
He departed thence to teach and preach in their cities...
(Matthew 11:1 KJV)

One day as he was teaching the people in the Temple courts and
preaching the gospel...
(Luke 20:1 NIV)

For additional references see: Matthew 4:17; Mark 1:38-39, 2:2, 6:12; Luke 4:43, 9:6; John 7:37-38, 18:20-21

While Jesus was still alive on the earth, He commissioned the Twelve for a preaching mission (Matthew 10:1-42). (See also: Mark 6:7-13 and Luke 9:1-6). By the time of His ascension into heaven and the subsequent empowerment of the Holy Spirit, these men had no doubt as to their God given assignment. Jesus had taught them well.

EXAMPLE/INSTRUCTION OF PAUL

For what do we best remember about the life of the Apostle Paul? Quite likely it was the three "missionary" journeys that he took. The purpose of these travels was to preach the Gospel of Christ and establish a New Testament church in each of the several locations. It is quite evident by his letters of guidance and instruction that these were "new converts". Even in written form, Paul was preaching/teaching divine Truth. Remember that these letters were later assembled into what we know today as the New Testament. All of this information came to these young believers as divine revelation by the Holy Spirit.

As Paul grew older, and the effects of his travels, along with the brutal persecution and imprisonment he endured, began to erode his energy and show in his body, he invested in younger men. Most notably, Timothy was mentored by the older man and given explicit instructions about ministry. The three word charge that Paul gave to his "son in the faith" has been used in ordination services for many years all around the world—"Preach the Word"

(2 Timothy 4:2). However, it should be noted that included in this final letter (2 Timothy) before his death, the great Apostle emphasizes the urgency of guarding the "doctrine." (Timothy is now pastor of the church at Ephesus.) It was not just that he preach, but that he knew what he was preaching. Yes, Timothy,

> *...study to show yourself approved unto God...rightly dividing the word of truth.*
> (2 Timothy 2:15 KJV)

> *...for "all Scripture is given by inspiration of God, and is profitable for doctrine, for reproof, for correction, for instruction in righteousness..."*
> (2 Timothy 3:16 KJV)

THREE

PURPOSE OF PREACHING IN THE NEW TESTAMENT

Evangelism—Salvation

John 3:16-17 is considered to be the theme verse for the entire Bible.

For God so loved the world that he gave his only begotten Son, that whosoever believeth in him should not perish, but have everlasting life. For God did not send his Son into the world to condemn the world; but that the world through him might be saved.

Luke concludes his account of the life and ministry of Christ with this message to the still confused disciples.

Yes, it was written long ago that the Messiah would suffer and die and rise from the dead on the third day. It was also written that this message would be proclaimed in the authority of his name to all the nations, beginning in Jerusalem. There is forgiveness of sins for all who repent.
(Luke 24:46-47 NLT)

Shortly after the Day of Pentecost, the Apostle Peter emphatically declared that Christ is the ONLY way to salvation.

For Jesus is the one referred to in the Scriptures, where it says: "The stone that you builders rejected has now become the cornerstone." There is salvation in no one else! God has given no other name by which we must be saved".
(Acts 4:11-12 NLT) (emphasis mine)

Throughout the writings of Paul, you can sense the full and

total commitment to preaching *"Christ and him crucified."* Such passages as—

> *For I am not ashamed of the gospel of Christ; for it is the power of God unto salvation to everyone that believeth...*
> (Romans 1:16 KJV)

Or, the passionate declaration to the young Corinthian church—

> *For the preaching of the cross is to them that perish foolishness; but unto us which are saved it is the power of God.*
> (1 Corinthians 1:18 KJV)

How can one not be moved by Paul's words concerning reconciliation?—

> *Anyone who belongs to Christ has become a new person. The old life is gone; a new life has begun!...and God has given us this task of reconciling people to him. For God was in Christ, reconciling the world to himself...For God made Christ, who never sinned, to be the offering for our sin, so that we could be made right with God through Christ.*
> (2 Corinthians 5:17-21 NLT)

Through the preaching of the Word, the Holy Spirit will reveal Christ as the one and onlyl way for depraved man with a sinful history to be given personal access into the presence of the eternally holy God.

God's grace is truly amazing!

The point is that as spokespersons for the Almighty, our first message must always be the glorious good news of forgiveness from sin and restoration to relationship with God by faith in Jesus Christ (Romans 5:1-2). There are many lessons to be learned in the daily walk of faith, but the beginning point is always a direct, personal, and crisis encounter with living Word! The message is not complicated, but it is profound! Never, ever lose sight of the Cross in your preaching.

SPIRITUAL GROWTH—SANCTIFICATION

It is most often the assignment of those called to be "Pastors" who must lead the people of God into a place of spiritual growth and maturity. For every believer this is a lifelong process. No one (including the pastor) ever reaches absolute perfection during this earthly sojourn. Day by day we strive against the minions of Satan whose goal is to push us back into the filthy pit of unbelief, disobedience, and blatant sin.

> Justification—the "formal acquittal" of our sins. At the moment of salvation we are positionally sanctified in Christ Jesus. (Romans 5:1-2)
>
> Sanctification—the process of "being conformed" to the image of Christ Jesus. Following salvation we are being progressively sanctified by the inner work of the Holy Spirit within. (2 Corinthians 3:18)

Paul clearly explains that it is the responsibility of the spiritual leaders (the gifts that Christ gave to His Church) to:

...equip God's people...to come to such unity of the faith and knowledge of God's Son that we will be mature in the Lord, measuring up to the full and complete standard of Christ. That we will no longer be immature like children...we will speak the truth in love, growing in every way more and more like Christ.
(Ephesians 4:11-16 NLT)

Peter admonishes believers to view themselves in the light of God's holiness.

As obedient children, do not conform to the evil desires you had when you lived in ignorance. But just as he who called you is holy, so be holy in all you do; for it is written: "Be holy, because I am holy."
(1 Peter 1:14-16 NIV)

Later, in his final letter before being put to death, Peter's very last comment reiterates the significance of the holy (sanctified) life.

But grow in the grace and knowledge of our Lord and Savior Jesus Christ.
(2 Peter 3:18 NIV)

No believer will ever be any stronger or more spiritually mature than his knowledge and personal application of the Word of God into daily living.

Helping followers of Christ achieve new levels of Scriptural understanding and subsequently encouraging the ongoing process of assimilating Truth into daily life is vital in fulfillment of the Great Commission. Jesus told His disciples to win the lost and then train them to serve Him.(Matthew 28:19-20)

Preacher, this is your assignment! Do it well!

Just as children must be taught—often by repetition, at times by discipline, always in love, with consistency in example—so those who are the children of God must grow from the *"milk"* to the *"meat"* of the Word (1 Corinthians 3:1-3).

DOCTRINAL TRUTH—SECURITY

Doctrine—a truth that is taught from a carefully developed set of principles, which are subsequently advocated by the adherents as guidelines for faith and practice.

Apologetics—defending (explaining) the doctrine (dogma, creed) of the Christian faith by using Scripture and illustrating with numerous empirical evidences from human history.

In His final recorded prayer for the Disciples (and us), our Lord prayed,

> *Sanctify them by the truth; your Word is truth.*
> (John 17:17 NIV)

It does matter what people believe.

1. Remember, a doctrinal truth is not derived from one verse of Scripture, but by what is taught in the entire Word of God.

2. Remember, that doctrinal error is often the result of selecting certain verses on a given subject, that are likely taken out of proper context, to prove a certain point.

3. Remember, that the Truth is found by (1) searching the entire Word of God, (2) understanding the original context of a passage, and (3) evaluation as being primarily God glorifying and Christ exalting.

With modern technological advances, it is possible for aberrant teaching to very quickly be passed around the globe. If the "flesh" is seeking to be "holy"; that is, the carnal desires of a sinful nature are being gratified under the disguise of Biblical revelation, the man of God must avoid accepting or advocating such teaching. Both Paul and Peter gave very solemn warnings about "false teachers and false prophets" bringing disruption and damaging confusion into the Body of Christ in the last days (Acts 20:27-31 and 2 Peter 2:1-22). To the "young ministers" of his day, Timothy and Titus, the Apostle Paul refers to the significance of maintaining Biblical doctrine approximately 15 times (1 & 2 Timothy and Titus).

Doctrinal error is often the result of an over-exaggeration of a given Biblical Truth, rather than being a complete departure from Scripture.

This exaggeration of Truth is more than likely the result of an under emphasis of that same Truth.

Any "new revelation" must be carefully evaluated in the bright light of ALL Scripture before it is accepted or proclaimed as Scriptural Truth.

FOUR

PERSONAL PREPARATION FOR MINISTRY: PREPARATION PRECEDES PRESENTATION

*P*rivate preparation validates public presentation. In short, what you do in private will determine the eternal results of your public ministry. The two cannot be separated.

> Men of God must emerge out of the darkness of the prayer closet into the glaring lights of humanity's desperate spiritual need and resolutely declare with unwavering certainty—"Thus saith the Lord!"

Having a charismatic personality or becoming a skilled orator will never substitute for waiting in the presence of God until He burns a message into your heart. Every time you step into the pulpit, your congregation should have full confidence that what you are saying is straight from the heart of God for them.

THE "MAN OF GOD" IS STILL ONLY A MAN

This sounds so very basic, almost redundant. Yes, God's grace fills my life. Yes, my past sins have been forgiven. But, none of us are perfect. Even our Lord Jesus was severely tempted after being baptized in water and then immediately fasting and praying for 40 days! (Matthew 4:1-11). Jesus was not out of the "will of God" when this temptation came.

"Turn stones into bread…"	Power over nature
"Leap from top of Temple…"	Authority over heavenly beings (angels)
"Bow down and worship Satan…"	Alternate plan for man's eternal redemption from sin

Although this is the most detailed of the temptations of Christ, remember that Satan only departed from Him for a period of time (Luke 4:13). In order to be "one of us," our Lord was *"tempted in every way, just as we are—yet was without sin"* (Hebrews 4:15 NIV). In the Garden of Gethsemane, just a few hours before the horrible crucifixion, the "man" Jesus, who had never sinned or disobeyed His Father, struggled with the reality that was before Him. His prayer? *"Father, if it is possible, let this cup (of death) pass from me..."* Simply, Jesus did not want to suffer this unjust death. We also know that He continued this intense prayer by declaring, *"Nevertheless, your will be done..."* (Matthew 26:36-46). He won the battle of the cross at that rock altar in Gethsemane and went directly from the private place of prayer to the mockery of a trail and cruel crucifixion.

The Apostle Paul knew that all he was came directly from the grace of God in his life.

> *For I (Paul) am the least of all the apostles. In fact, I'm not even worthy to be called an apostle after the way I persecuted God's church. But whatever I am now, it is all because God poured out his special favor on me—and not without results...it was not I but God who was working through me by his grace.*
> (1 Corinthians 15:9-10 NLT)

We must constantly remind ourselves that once we have declared our position as an "ambassador" for Christ Jesus, Satan and all of his minions will unleash the full arsenal of hell against us. This is no game. You, the threat to invade the territory of darkness, become a prime target. There is nothing that Satan likes better than to bring to shame one who proclaims Christ as God's Son and man's only Redeemer (2 Timothy 3:12).

> *If you think you are standing strong, be careful not to fall. The temptations in your life are no different from what others experience. And God is faithful: He will not allow the temptation to be more than you can stand. When you are tempted, he will show you a way out so that you can endure.*
> (1 Corinthians 10:12-13 NLT)

By the grace of God we are "more than conquerors" in Christ Jesus (Romans 8:37)!

RECOGNIZE/RESIST SINFUL ENTICEMENTS

It is true that Satan is a deceiver. Perhaps two of the most frequent overt, externally observable sins among spiritual leaders relate to money and morals. Repeatedly, the Scripture gives warning of the dangers of being caught in such traps. Unfortunately many of the Old Testament examples are of those chosen to be spiritual leaders (i.e. Eli's sons—1 Samuel 2:22-36). Statistics of those who were once in the ministry, but are no longer qualified to be a spiritual leader, will verify that the vast majority of them were guilty of financial dishonesty or moral impurity.

Read Paul's letters to his "son in the faith" Timothy. Paul's counsel to young Timothy is solemn—and certainly applicable for today's spiritual leaders.

Of the lure of desiring more earthly things:

Yet true godliness with contentment is itself great wealth. So if we have enough food and clothing, let us be content. For the love of money is the root of all kinds of evil.
(1 Timothy 6:6-10 NLT)

Of the destructive nature of sexual impurity (fornication, adultery, incest, homosexuality):

Do not share in the sins of others. Keep yourself pure.
(1 Timothy 5:22 NLT)

If you keep yourself pure, you will be a special utensil for honorable use. Your life will be clean and you will be ready for the Master to use you for every good work. Run from anything that stimulates youthful lusts.
(2 Timothy 2:21-22 NLT)

It cannot be overstated as to the severity of the damage that results when a man of God yields to such temptation. Not only

is there sorrow, shame, dishonor and heartache for the individual minister and his family, but also to the larger Body of Christ.
Unbelieving skeptics are given yet another excuse to heap shame
and ridicule upon the cause of Jesus Christ. The Holy Spirit is
faithful to place warning signs in our pathway and show us that
to proceed in that direction will surely bring personal and ministerial disaster. If we fall into such open sin it is because we did
not (1) honestly recognize our own human weakness, (2) resist
(take a military stance against) the Devil, nor (3) appropriate
the grace of God available to help us overcome temptations.

SUBTLE DETERRENTS TO EFFECTIVE MINISTRY

1 LACK OF HUMILITY One might say that pride has the same
meaning, as it is certainly the opposite of humility. To be certain,
from the Garden of Eden temptation to the future coming of the
anti-Christ, pride has been at the core of sinful actions. Warning
after warning is given in Scripture to avoid pride or to quickly repent of it when it finds lodging in the heart. Pride is the threshold
to spiritual disaster.

> *Pride goes before destruction, and haughtiness before a fall.*
> (Proverbs 16:18 NLT)

Allow me to explain the distinction that I see between pride
and the lack of humility. By definition, humility is to consider
one's self unworthy. So, if I reach a point where I am comfortable or content in the assumed effectiveness of how I "perform"
in the ministry, I may not be arrogant or self consumed, just not
understanding or regarding my total unworthiness. Never, ever
lose sight of the One who has called and enabled you to be His
servant. All else is ancillary and must be viewed through the lens
of our Lord's worthiness. Without Christ we are absolutely nothing and our charismatic personality or oratorical skills will please
only the flesh.

Paul spoke often of his sense of unworthiness to be the Lord's messenger. From Philippians 3 we learn that he was highly educated, a Pharisee who had earned great respect among his peers as a skilled teacher of the Old Testament law. Saul (before his name was changed to Paul) was a man of great influence in the Jewish religion and culture. People listened to what he had to say. Yet, after coming into contact with the living Christ, he declares all of this—his heritage, his training, his talent, his adherence to Jewish tradition—to be worthless garbage, only to be thrown away (Philippians 3:4-11).

I am the least of all the apostles...
(1 Corinthians 15:9 NLT)

My life is worth nothing to me unless I use it for finishing the work assigned to me by the Lord Jesus—
(Acts 20:24 NLT)

② **ABUSE OF AUTHORITY** There is an old proverb which says, "If you really want to know a man's character, give him a position of authority." Jesus taught that true leaders are servants—not "masters." At the last meal (Lord's Supper) before Jesus went to the cross, in a dramatic move He took the place of a lowly household servant and washed the disciples' feet (John 13:4-16). In coordinating the timing of events recorded by the four (4) Gospel writers, many scholars believe that at this very moment the Disciples were still debating about position and prominence in the restored Kingdom of Israel (Luke 22:19-24). This was a powerful teaching moment. Jesus emphasized that spiritual leaders were to serve—an attitude that was in stark contradiction to the philosophy of a self serving culture. By the way, there is no record that these Disciples were ever again embroiled in a debate about their personal importance in positions of leadership after the Day of Pentecost.

The servant of the Lord must "not strive" (2 Timothy 2:24) to always be in control of every situation. Some things are of such insignificance in the eternal scheme that it is reproachful for the man of God to become embroiled in trivial matters.

❸ ENVIOUS OF OTHER'S SUCCESS King Saul became envious of David after he killed Goliath. As the army was returning home after this great victory over the Philistines, the woman along the parade route sang,

> It is much easier to hurt with another who is suffering in some difficult situation than it is to rejoice with one who has just experienced a tremendous accomplishment.
>
> This is human nature, and it must be nailed to the cross!

Saul has killed his thousands, and David his ten thousands. This made Saul very angry...so from that time on Saul kept a jealous eye on David.
(1 Samuel 18:6-9 NLT)

This Old Testament story recounts that King Saul tried to personally kill David, and even sent his best military men into the wilderness to find and kill him. He was consumed by this evil spirit of jealousy. Ultimately, King Saul was killed in disgrace and David became the king of Israel.

As you review the ministry of the four major Old Testament prophets, you will recall that three of them—Jeremiah, Ezekiel, and Daniel—were contemporaries. There is no Scriptural indication that one was envious of the other. Jeremiah was thrown into a pit and sank in mud up to his arm pits, but you never hear him muttering about how unfair his plight is, while a younger Daniel is living in the king's palace.

You make deep and painful sacrifices for the work of the Lord—it seems that there are almost no visible results. You earnestly pray—your prayers seem to never leave the room. On and on it goes. Yet, there is a brother that whatever he attempts to do is overwhelmingly successful. People are always pointing to his newest accomplishment. You know that you work as hard as he does. He must have someone in authority to push him forward. Or, surely he compromises the message to have such a large following. If you become obsessed with another's recognition or position, it will haunt your mind and spirit. To say the very least, your effectiveness in accomplishing God's plan for your life will be diminished. Before you allow that spirit to invade your thoughts, remember the cruel, unjust jealousy that was directed toward our Lord. Those who should have welcomed and supported His ministry were intent on putting the Messiah to death.

④ FEAR OF FAILURE To say "I can't do this" in reference to what God has called us to do is, at the very least, an expression of a lack of trust in the sovereign wisdom of the Almighty. We often speak about how Peter began to sink as he saw the waves rolling all around him. Surely, we conclude, it was a "lack of faith" on his part. But, remember, Peter did get out of the boat! He responded to the Lord's bidding, while the other disciples remained huddled in the boat terrified by what was happening around them. (Matthew 14:22-33; Mark 6:45-52: John 6:15-21)

There is an important distinction between acting in faith and being presumptuous. Foolish decisions, outside of the Spirit's guidance, have created many disasters. Which, in turn, have fostered a paralyzing fear about going forward. The spiritual leader must first hear the voice of God, respond accordingly and responsibly, and then solemnly commit the future results into His hands.

The army of the Lord is not simply marching in place—we are charging forward into the enemy's territory, destroying his strongholds, and raising the blood stained banner of the Cross.

I have strength for all things in Christ Who empowers me {I am ready for anything and equal to anything through Him Who infuses inner strength into me; I am self sufficient in Christ's sufficiency}.
(Philippians 4:13 AMP)

Doubt questions if God can—Fear questions if God will.

One says that God is unable—the other that God is unwilling.

Fear causes the minister to say "I cannot…" because he believes that "God will not."

5 **THE OPINION OF OTHERS** We all need counsel and advice from the spiritually mature. The fact is that even the most intelligent will not always have all the correct answers. God will use others to strengthen our hands in His service, just as Aaron and Hur held up the hands of Moses during the battle with the Amalekites in Rephidim (Exodus 17:8-16). Simply said, as spiritual leaders, we must be surrounded by faithful men and women who share in the vision that God has given us. Never take an adversarial role toward them. Their prayers, presence, and partnership are vital to advancing the cause of Jesus Christ in any location in the world.

Having said that, the thought of section relates to exactly the opposite scenario. People who constantly criticize, find fault, and gossip about who we are and what we are attempting to do for the Kingdom can bring us to a place of despair and discouragement very quickly. The natural tendencies are two: (1) To fight back—to defend ourselves, or (2) to run away—just abandon the mission. However, to yield to either of these approaches is harmful to us as individuals, as well as bringing confusion in the Body of Christ.

Paul to Timothy:

> *Again I say, don't get involved in foolish, ignorant arguments that only start fights. A servant of the Lord must not quarrel but must be kind to everyone, be able to teach, and be patient with difficult people.*
> (2 Timothy 2:23-24 NLT)

For the man chosen to lead the people of God, it is absolutely mandatory to be introspectively honest. When criticism is hurled like a flaming arrow to the heart, we should very carefully evaluate the veracity of such comments. If they are correct, and we have fallen short of God's plan in some area, every attempt should be made to rectify the situation as quickly as possible. In other words, it must not be our own failure or spiritually immaturity that bring about stinging remarks (1 Peter 4:12-16). However, when you have prayerfully and honestly determined that the criticism is not valid, by the grace of God it should be put aside. Peacefully and joyfully proceed in the work of the Lord!

After declaring to the believers at Corinth that he has "this great treasure (salvation in Christ) in a fragile clay jar," Paul defines the pressures of ministerial life and the response that is enabled by the power of Christ living within.

> *We are pressed on every side by troubles, but we are not crushed.*
> *We are perplexed, but not driven to despair. We are hunted*
> *down, but never abandoned by God. We get knocked down, but*
> *we are not destroyed.*
> (2 Corinthians 4:7-9 NLT)

Twice in this chapter, Paul proclaims that he will *"never give up"* (2 Corinthians 4:1, 16 NLT) in this journey to eternity.

Jesus put the seriousness of committed discipleship in simple agricultural terms:

> *No one who puts his hand to the plow and looks back is fit for*
> *service in the kingdom of God.*
> (Luke 9:62 NIV)

Jesus willingly (1) left His exalted place at the Father's right hand; (2) humbled Himself to live in a human body, (3) restricted His own deity, (4) went to the cross for our sin, and (5) made it possible for us to enter into a peaceful, restored relationship with God the Father. Could what anyone would ever think or say about or against us as His chosen disciples diminish or negate the love we have for our Lord? It is impossible to "pay" for our salvation, but it is not too much to ask that we keep our hearts and eyes

> *...focused on what lies ahead...to reach the end of the race and receive*
> *the heavenly prize for which God, through Christ Jesus, is calling us.*
> (Philippians 3:13-14 NLT)

6 RESENTMENT FOR PERSONAL SACRIFICES Gehazi, the servant of the prophet Elisha, just could not comprehend that Naaman would return to Syria with all the "gifts" that he had tried to present to Elisha after being healed of leprosy (2 Samuel 5:20-27). Gehazi was young. He saw a quick, easy way to have some "nice things". At that moment, the temptation for a better lifestyle overcame him. In addition to the greed that crept into his heart, it is quite possible that Gehazi had been living a very modest life with the prophet. No doubt he saw others who enjoyed more comfortable surroundings. Over time, resentment may have been crouching in some dark corner of his heart. "I deserve better than this." "I work as hard as he does—look at all that he has." "God has not been fair with me." On and on the demonic voices from hell torment the mind. And, then like all "hidden" sin, at the precise moment it will strike like a poisonous snake hidden deep in the grass.

You will never be content with the place you have been called to serve in ministry, so long as you consider sacrifice as sacrifice!

Colleague in His service, remember that your reward does not come in the perishable things of this earth such as silver and gold. These are not our real treasures. Not only will they pass away, but they cannot be taken into eternity (Matthew 6:19-21). In fact, earthly possessions will seem cheap and imperfect once we enter the gates of pearl and walk on the eternal streets of Gold. The most glorious reward for service will be when we hear:

Well done, my good and faithful servant. You have been faithful in handling this small amount, so now I will give you many more responsibilities. Let's celebrate together!
(Matthew 25:21, 23 NLT)

FIVE

PREACH THE WORD

*T*he Word of God is the basis for eternal truth.

Word is INSPIRED (2 Timothy 3:15-16; 2 Peter 1:19-21)

Word is INFALLIBLE (Psalm 119:89; Matthew 24:35)

Word is ETERNAL (Isaiah 40:8; Matthew 5:18)

The proclamation of the Word of God, from Genesis to Revelation, is intended to reveal the character and nature of God to His creation. As you study the Word, it becomes clear that through each portion of man's history, God is progressively revealing Himself and the plan of eternal redemption that came through the Lord Jesus Christ. As Paul says,

...the Law was our school teacher to bring us to Jesus Christ.
(Galatians 3:24 KJV)

Grace and truth came by Jesus Christ.
(John 1:17 KJV)

The dynamic power of the Word is that it touches every aspect of man's being (Hebrews 4:12). It is generally understood that there are three (3) components in man's decision making—Intellect, Emotions, and Will.

The Word CHALLENGES THE INTELLECT

The Word CHARGES THE EMOTIONS

The Word CHANGES THE WILL

The ultimate theme of Biblical preaching is Christ's sacrificial and substitutionary provision for all mankind to be restored to a loving relationship with the heavenly Father.

The Old Testament prophetically anticipates.

The New Testament propositionally proclaims.

SEE THE BIG PICTURE OF SCRIPTURE

The Scriptures, both Old and New Testament, are verbally inspired by God, the revelation of God to men, the infallible, authoritative rule of faith and conduct. (2 Timothy 3:15-17; 2 Peter 1:21)

The Bible was written over a period of 1600 years, by more than 40 different authors.

Old Testament		New Testament	
39 Books	32 plus authors	27 Books	8 plus authors
One central theme: Men's redemption through Christ Jesus.			

God's plan is progressively revealed in Scripture:

Genesis—Character/Nature of God (first 2,500 years of history)

Exodus-Malachi—Law of Moses

Gospels—Christ as Son of men/Son of God

Acts—Holy Spirit out poured, New Testament Church

Romans-Jude—Ministry to Church on earth

Revelation—Final, complete revelation of God

Scripture reveals God to men as being:

Omnipotent—All powerful

Omniscient—All wise, knowing

Omnipresent—All (everywhere) present

God in relationship to His moral creation is declared to be:

Love

Holiness

Truth

OLD TESTAMENT DIVISIONS	
PENTATEUCH	FIRST FIVE BOOKS—WRITTEN BY MOSES
Genesis	The book of origins. Creation, fall of men, Man's redemption, Adam/Eve, Noah, Abraham and his descendants. Approximately 2,500 years.
Exodus	Egyptian bondage, deliverance (exodus), journey on the way to Canaan.
Leviticus	The book of laws concerning morals, foods, cleanliness. Holiness before the Lord is the theme.
Numbers	The 40 years in the wilderness (only 2nd and 40th year recorded).
Deuteronomy	Moses final five sermons to the Israelites, repetition of the law before entering the Promised Land.
HISTORICAL BOOKS	12 IN NUMBER—VARIOUS AUTHORS
Joshua	The conquest of Canaan, under Joshua's leadership, with the division of land among the 12 Tribes of Israel.
Judges	History of the six servitudes of Israel, with various deliverances, under 15 judges. Often called "The Dark Ages" of Israel.
Ruth	A beautiful love story in with Ruth (a Gentile) enters into the direct ancestry of David (and Jesus Christ).

OLD TESTAMENT DIVISIONS	
1 & 2 Samuel	History of the judge Samuel, and the monarchy of Saul and David.
1 & 2 Kings	History of the Kingdom (12 tribes) and then the Northern (10 Tribes) & Southern Kingdoms (2 Tribes).
1 & 2 Chronicles	Basically the record of David, Solomon, and subsequent kings of Judah, until the time of the Babylonian captivity.
Ezra	A record of the return of the Jews from captivity and the rebuilding of the Temple in Jerusalem.
Nehemiah	An account of the rebuilding the walls of Jerusalem and reestablishing the sacred ordinances.
Esther	Story of Esther, the Jewish queen that God raised up and then used to deliver the Jews from destruction.
POETICAL BOOKS	FIVE BOOKS—VARIOUS AUTHORS
Job	Believed to be the oldest manuscript, unveils the problems of affliction/suffering as it relates to the plan and purposes of God. The vanity of human understanding in comparison with Divine Wisdom is shown.
Psalms	A magnificent collection of spiritual songs, poems, and prayers used by both Jews and Christians for worship.
Proverbs	A collection of moral guidelines and discourses on wisdom, justice, temperance, and many other subjects, penned by King Solomon.
Ecclesiastes	The vanity of human search for true happiness in the present life, with conclusion of man's duty to God.

OLD TESTAMENT DIVISIONS	
Song of Solomon	An allegory symbolizing the mutual love of Christ and the Church's love for Christ.
PROPHETIC BOOKS	17 BOOKS, WITH FOUR CLASSIFIED AS MAJOR, 12 AS MINOR (ONE MAJOR PROPHET WROTE A SECOND BOOK)
Isaiah (major)	The prophet of redemption, Messianic prophecies, primarily to North Kingdom, but also to other sinful nations.
Jeremiah (major)	"The Weeping Prophet" spoke to Southern Kingdom, (in Jerusalem) warned of captivity because of idol worship, but gave hope of restoration.
Lamentations (second book by Jeremiah)	A series of "lamentings" because of the afflictions of Israel.
Ezekiel (major)	Many illustrated sermons, often speaks exactly the words the Lord instructs him. Ministered to Jewish captives in Babylon.
Daniel (major)	A personal biography, plus visions of future events. Ministered from palace in Babylon.
Hosea (minor)	The sad story of Hosea's personal life, as an illustration of the unfaithfulness of God's people to Him.
Joel (minor)	Major emphasis is "The Day of the Lord" which will be both a time of judgment and blessing. Often referred to as "The prophet of Pentecost."
Amos (minor)	Spoke against injustice/selfishness. The book contains a series of five visions.
Obadiah (minor)	The doom of Edom (descendants of Esau) and the deliverance of Israel.

OLD TESTAMENT DIVISIONS	
Jonah (minor)	Personal biography of the prophet who learned the value of obedience to the Sovereign Lord.
Micah (minor)	Presents the sinful condition of God's people, but foretells the establishment of the Messianic Kingdom in which righteousness will prevail.
Nahum (minor)	The doom of Nineveh. Nahum prophesied about 150 years after Jonah when Nineveh repented.
Habakkuk (minor)	Questions concerning the justice of God. Why does God allow His people to suffer under the hand of evil people? God reveals the day of coming victory.
Zephaniah (minor)	The solemn warning of judgment for Judah and other sinful nations. Promise of restoration to come.
Haggai (minor)	Encouraged the Jewish people to rebuild the Temple after 15 years of doing nothing. Promise of an even greater Temple in the future.
Zechariah (minor)	Encouraged the rebuilding of the Temple. A series of 8 visions, expressing ultimate triumph of God's Kingdom.
Malachi (minor)	A graphic picture of the closing of this period in Jewish history, with promise of the coming Messiah.

NEW TESTAMENT DIVISIONS	
BIOGRAPHICAL BOOKS	FOUR BOOKS, FOUR AUTHORS, CALLED THE "GOSPELS." MATTHEW, MARK, AND LUKE ARE CALLED THE SYNOPTIC GOSPELS BECAUSE MUCH OF THE MATERIAL IN ONE IS ALSO FOUND IN THE OTHER TWO.

NEW TESTAMENT DIVISIONS

Matthew	Christ depicted as Messiah, written primarily to a Jewish audience, speaks frequently of the "Kingdom".
Mark	Christ depicted as Servant of God and man, with many illustrations of the power of God at work through Christ. Believed to be a close friend of Simon Peter.
Luke	Christ depicted as Son of Man, with more of the words of Christ than the other writers. Luke was a medical doctor, the only Gentile writer in Scripture, and a close associate of Paul.
John	Christ depicted as Son of God, mostly recording events/teaching not found in the other Gospels. Jesus refers to God as His "Father" numerous times.

The church of the twenty-first century is part of the New Testament church which began at Pentecost.

The New Testament church began with the outpouring of the Holy Spirit as promised by Christ...and continues today with the Holy Spirit at work collectively in the body of believers and individually in believers.

The baptism in the Holy Spirit (Acts 2:4), the gifts of the Spirit (1 Corinthians 12:4-11), and the fruit of the Spirit (Galatians 5:22-23) must be expressed and evident in the New Testament church of this generation.

NEW TESTAMENT DIVISIONS

HISTORICAL BOOK	ONE BOOK, AUTHORED BY LUKE
Acts	The birth and growth of the New Testament Church is documented, primarily from the Day of Pentecost to Paul's imprisonment in Rome.

NEW TESTAMENT DIVISIONS	
PAULINE LETTERS AND EPISTLES	14 IN NUMBER (IF YOU INCLUDE THE BOOK OF HEBREWS)
Romans	Considered to be one of the finest literary writings by both sacred and secular scholars. Addressed to Roman Christians, the book contains a powerful exposition of the need for, the nature of, and the exclusive plan of salvation (justification by faith).
1 Corinthians	To the church Paul founded on his 2nd missionary journey, he addresses a variety of evils/factions in this "immature" body of believers.
2 Corinthians	Paul is defending his apostleship. In this personal letter, he reveals much about his philosophy of ministry
Galatians	Warning about those who required keeping the ceremonial Law of Moses in addition to Christ for salvation. Again, he emphasizes the doctrine of justification by faith.
Ephesians	A powerful plea for unity in the body of Christ, emphasizing that all barriers have been broken in Christ.
Philippians	A "Thank You" letter to the church for their financial gifts to him. Although written from prison in Rome, "Joy" and "Rejoicing" are recurrent themes.
Colossians	Paul show that Christ is "Head of Church" and that all worldly philosophies/sin are to be abandoned.
1 Thessalonians	Paul explains the comfort and hope found in looking for the soon return of Christ.

NEW TESTAMENT DIVISIONS	
2 Thessalonians	As a sequel to the first letter, Paul writes to clarify some misunderstandings about the "coming of the Lord".
1 Timothy	Instruction/counsel from an older minister to his "son in the faith."
2 Timothy	Paul's final letter before his execution in Rome. Encouragement, counsel, instruction are given to the young pastor.
Titus	Encouragement to a friend who is serving in a very difficult place. Works are emphasized in this letter.
Philemon	A private letter to his friend Philemon, encouraging him to receive and forgive Onesimus, a runaway slave, who has been converted.
Hebrews	Some question about the authorship of this epistle; however, many scholars believe that Paul wrote it because of its detailed references to the Law. The "old" is compared with the "new" showing that Christ is "better."
GENERAL EPISTLES	SEVEN IN NUMBER, BY FOUR AUTHORS
James	Most likely the half brother of Jesus. A very practical book with emphasis on combining faith and works.
1 Peter	Letter of encouragement written to the churches throughout Asia Minor. Believed that it was written shortly after Paul was executed. Theme is "Victory in Suffering."
2 Peter	Letter of warning against false teachers in the church.

NEW TESTAMENT DIVISIONS	
1 John	Deep message on relationships, fellowship and love, especially among believers.
2 John	Brief message on heresy and false teachers.
3 John	A personal message to Gaius, along with character sketches of others in the church.
Jude	Brief message of warning against apostasy, false teachers and the coming judgment of God.
PROPHETIC BOOK	ONE BOOK, AUTHORED BY JOHN THE APOSTLE (WHO ALSO WROTE THE GOSPEL OF JOHN, PLUS 1,2, & 3 JOHN).
Revelation	Focuses on seven local churches in Asia Minor and then describes the final "revelation" of Jesus Christ.

If possible, have a good translation of the Bible in your language, with a concordance (an alphabetical list of the words and the Scripture passage where each word may be found) and study notes.

UNDERSTAND THE CONTEXT OF TEXT PASSAGE

This requires some study and research; however, this will be extremely beneficial in the preacher's preparation of the sermon. To adequately understand the context of a given book or passage of Scripture, you should be able to answer the following questions:

1. Who is the author of this book?

2. When was it written? (i.e. during the Kingdom years of Israel, New Testament Church era, etc.)

3. What were the circumstances when the book was written? (i.e. Paul in prison, Israel in captivity in

Babylon, etc.)

4. To whom was it written? (i.e. children of Israel, local church in New Testament, etc.)

5. What is the overall message of the book/passage? (i.e. judgment for sin, future events, etc.)

6. What is the major theme of the book?

7. What are the unique features of this book? (i.e. style in which it was written, etc.)

In all probability you will not include all, or even most, of this information when you deliver the sermon. However, by providing some aspects of the original situation, the congregation will be able to more easily comprehend the writer's intent. This will also assist

> Ministers of the Gospel do not consider serious study of the Word to be a burdensome chore.
>
> Those who would be effective in the pulpit recognize that searching the word is a lifelong privilege, which results in the holy spirit's revelation of humanly incomprehensible truth.

the preacher in connecting the passage to current times/events and cultural mores when the application is being made.

Maintain Scriptural Integrity

God is serious about the integrity of His own Word!

> *For ever, O Lord, thy word is settled in heaven.*
> (Psalm 119:89 KJV)

> *The grass withers and the flowers fall, but the word of our God stands forever.*
> (Isaiah 40:7 NIV)

I tell you the truth, until heaven and earth disappear, not the smallest letter, not the least stroke of a pen, will by any means disappear from the Law until everything is accomplished. Anyone who breaks one of the least of these commandments and teaches others to do the same will be called least in the kingdom of heaven; but whoever practices and teaches these commands will be called great in the kingdom of heaven.

(Matthew 5:18-19 NIV—Jesus)

God says what He means—and means what He says!

And I solemnly declare to everyone who hears the words of prophecy written in this book: If anyone adds anything to what is written here, God will add to that person the plagues described in this book. And if anyone removes any of the words from this book of prophecy, God will remove that person's share in the tree of life and in the holy city that are described in this book.

(Revelation 22:18-19 NLT)

Man of God, do not get caught up in the most recent popular "revelation." Some teachers may be able to attract large numbers of people, but afterward the landscape is littered with wounded spirits and disillusioned seekers. To exploit people for any reason is evil, but to pervert the Word of God for personal gain and selfish ambition is never overlooked by the Almighty. Remember, He will not share His own glory with another. Before you preach something that you heard another minister say, be absolutely cer-

God does not need for any man to "defend Him. His Word is true and will never fail. Consequently, the preacher should never make "promises" that are different or other than the promises in God's Word.

Since God's ways/thoughts are higher than our ways/thoughts, human wisdom is incapable of comprehending or explaining the wisdom/ actions of the eternal one (Romans 11:33; 1 Corinthians 2:1-9).

tain that it can be verified by the Word of God. Paul gives some sage advice.

Prove all things. Hold fast that which is good.

(1 Thessalonians 5:21 KJV)

RELY ON THE HOLY SPIRIT'S ANOINTING

The word "anoint" is primarily an Old Testament word, which in the Hebrew implies to consecrate for an office or ministry (i.e., Aaron as High Priest, David to become king, etc.). Literally, it means to "rub" or "smear." Although in the Old Testament it was an actual event with a special anointing oil, it was also a symbolic gesture of God's call, approval, and empowerment of the individual.

Jesus read from the Prophet Isaiah (61:1-3) at the beginning of His earthly ministry and stated that the *"anointing"* from God for ministry was upon Him (Luke 6:16-21). There was no vial of oil poured over the head of our Lord, but this public announcement was validated repeatedly during the next 3 years by His preaching, teaching, healing of the sick, and many other miracles. Jesus, in some fashion, limited His own deity while in the flesh and did these mighty works in and through the power of the Holy Spirit. Our Lord told the Disciples:

> *He that believeth on me, the works that I do shall he do also; and greater works than these shall he do; because I go unto the Father.*
> (John 14:12 KJV)

In the context of this passage, Christ was telling the disciples He would soon be leaving this world—but that He would send the Holy Spirit to anoint and enable them. Simply, it would be the power of the Holy Spirit that would empower them to do His work. He again confirmed this after the resurrection, by telling them to go to Jerusalem.

> *I send the promise of my Father upon you: but tarry ye in the city of Jerusalem, until ye be endued with power from on high.*
> (Luke 24:49; also Acts 1:8 KJV)

The challenge for men of God today who respond to God's call and sense His approval is to recognize and receive the Holy Spirit's empowerment. While it is always appropriate to strive for excellence in our service to the Lord, it is only by the power of the Holy Spirit's anointing upon our lives that we are able to minister in the supernatural realm. Do you recall the story of the seven sons of Sceva who tried to cast out demons—without the power of the Holy Spirit (Acts 19:13-17)? All seven were overpowered by one man filled with evil spirits! That is a good lesson for us to remember. Satan is never willing to relinquish any of his "territory" (John 12:31, 14:30; 2 Corinthians 4:4; Ephesians 2:2) and will unleash the forces of Hell to come against the minister of the Gospel. Jesus overcame the Devil in the wilderness temptation with the Word of God—three verses from the Book of Deuteronomy! Of the challenges that Satan gave to Christ, the greatest was for Him to bow down and worship Satan. And, if Christ would do so, then Satan would give Him

> *the glory of these kingdoms and authority over them, because they are mine to give to anyone I please. I will give it all to you if you will worship me.*
> (Luke 4:5-7 NLT)

Satan was offering Christ an "easier" way to rule over the earth. Literally, the father of lies was telling Christ you do not have to go to the Cross!

How do we today overcome such attacks? By the anointing of the Holy Spirit upon our lives!! This is true both in the out of the pulpit.

SIX

HOW WILL YOU PRESENT THE MESSAGE?

PREACH WHAT YOU HAVE PERSONALLY EXPERIENCED

It is impossible to preach/teach about the faith life in Christ if you have not personally experienced salvation? Can you encourage others to be filled with the Baptism in the Holy Spirit as taught in Acts 2:4, if you have never had this powerful experience? What about miracles? Or, deliverance? Have you prayed the prayer of faith and witnessed divine intervention into a circumstance that was beyond human resources? Preacher, stay close to Christ! Stay full of the Holy Spirit! God wants to use you as His chosen vessel to advance the eternal plan of redemption.

PREACH WITH PASSION AND COMPASSION

PASSION—intense emotion which powerfully impacts another; unwavering belief in proposition.

This could be defined as one's life controlling conviction—from which there is no compromise. It is a belief held so strongly that even the threat of death will not elicit a retraction. An opinion (what I think) on a given subject can be altered. A conviction (which supersedes argument or logic) is integrated into the very fiber of character and refuses to be swayed by cultural opinion.

Paul was not only willing *"to be jailed at Jerusalem but even to die for the sake of the Lord Jesus"* (Acts 21:13 NLT).

Preaching must be persuasive. The preacher must believe—without any reservation—every word that he preaches. He must preach in a manner so there can be no questions about his commitment to the authority of God's Word.

49

COMPASSION—intense emotion for the suffering, pain of others; deep sympathy.

The Gospels depict Christ as a man of great compassion. A frequent observation by the writers was that Jesus was "moved with compassion"—on the multitudes, on the confused people of Israel, on the sick and diseased, on the poor, on those struggling with crisis situations, on those marginalized by society (i.e. several passages in Matthew, Mark, and Luke).

It is easy to become desensitized to pain and suffering by what is commonly seen around us. Worse yet, is to become critical and cynical. One man said, "If you are angry and willing that people should go to hell, you should not preach about it."

> People do not care how much you know—until they know how much you care!

On occasion I have been asked, "What is the single most important piece of advice you would give to a young minister?" For me, the answer is simple. Love people. If you have a heart filled with compassion, people will desire for you to minister to them. By the way, the minister (servant) earns the respect of people by the way he treats them when he is not in the pulpit. They will listen to his sermons because they have seen his heart!

ADVANCE PREPARATION IS IMPORTANT

There are occasions when you may be asked to preach with only a few minutes advance notice. And, of course, the Holy Spirit will direct you to the portion of God's Word that is needed by that particular audience. So, in our hearts we must be prepared at all times to share the Truth. However, especially for the pastor who stands in the same pulpit week after week, preaching/teaching to the same congregation, he must spend large amounts of time in preparing the message. To do so is very valuable for both the pastor and the church family.

✓ The Holy Spirit knows well "in advance" of the day you preach who will be in the congregation. He is not surprised by those who are present on Sunday morning!

✓ Preparing "in advance" prevents repetition of certain Biblical truths (as important as they may be) to the exclusion of other equally important doctrinal truths. Knowing what you preached last Sunday or last month is very important for the Pentecostal (full Gospel) preacher!

✓ Preparing "in advance" allows time for the preacher (1) to understand the context of the passage, (2) search for clarification of the meaning of the text, (3) coordinate other Scriptures to confirm, explain, and amplify the truth that is to be presented, and (4) absorb the Truth of this message into his own spirit.

✓ Preparing "in advance" lends itself to preaching a "series" (several consecutive messages) on a given subject. For example: Lessons from the Life of King David, or the Book of James (on practical Christian living), or The Events of the Passion of Christ, or The Sermon on the Mount. The list for such preaching series is endless—but to be effective and meaningful, there must be extensive, prayerful preparation.

✓ The worshippers will come to God's House expecting to receive insight into the Word of God when they know that you have prepared *"in advance"* to stand in the pulpit and with holy boldness declare, *"Thus saith the Lord."*

UNDERSTAND THE SPIRITUAL MATURITY OF THE AUDIENCE

Jesus spoke to the multitudes (untrained in Rabbinical Law) in very simple terms. He often used parables to illustrate a spiritual truth. Yet, on the other hand, He reached for another level of understanding with His disciples. To the Jewish religious leaders, Jesus was often very direct in challenging their behavior for seeking recognition and personal influence, rather than desiring to show the love of God for His people.

The Apostle Peter instructs spiritual leaders to very gently and lovingly "care for the flock"in the following manner—"feed," "nurture," "protect," and "lead" (1 Peter 5:1-4).

Perhaps Peter is recalling the analogy that Jesus made concerning Himself as the "Good Shepherd" and "His sheep" (John 10:1-18).

The Holy Spirit is very faithful to reveal the spiritual needs of his congregation to the earnest pastor. Growing is vital to the life of every believer. Infants, become toddlers; who, in turn, become young children, then teenagers. The process continues until these babies become mature and responsible adults. If the Word of God is preached with clarity, in a similar spiritual manner there will be continuing spiritual development in the community of faith.

There are only two options in the Christian experience—either you are growing or you are dying...You cannot remain the same!

SEVEN

CHOOSING THE RIGHT METHOD
FOR THE MESSAGE:
MANY STYLES OF SERMON PRESENTATION

God uses individual personalities to accomplish His work. Consider the individual uniqueness of the prophets Elijah and Elisha. One a rugged outdoorsman, the other a docile farmer. Certainly the distinction in the personalities of Peter and Paul are obvious—one a converted fisherman, the other a converted scholar of Rabbinical Law. Or, one may look at how Barnabas ("Son of Encouragement") was used to assist in the development of the younger believers (including Paul and John Mark).

Especially in the New Testament, a quick overview of the writers (total of 8) will clearly reveal that each had a unique "style" of writing. They were all inspired by the Holy Spirit. The Spirit did not nullify their personality; rather, He anointed and used it for the glory of God.

God did not call you to imitate another preacher's style. Over the years I have observed some young preachers who wanted to preach like a famous preacher. They would modify their own voice to sound like that person, try to use similar gestures, and even repeat phrases that were frequently used by the well known minister. It is not effective. God chose you and He will equip you—anoint your personality. God is sending you forth with a message from eternity. Allow Him to use your uniqueness in delivering the Word.

Use Variety to Communicate More Effectively

In the ensuing pages, I have listed four prominent types of sermon presentations. They will be defined, with examples of that particular style of approach to preaching. Any sermon "style" or "outline" is only a tool to assist in delivering the message in a manner that can be remembered by the hearers. There is nothing sacred about how long or short or even if you have written "notes" when you enter the pulpit.

It is valuable to use a variety of styles and approaches to the sermon presentation. This will keep the congregation engaged and will allow you to avoid repetition. Listed here are a few suggestions that could perhaps be included from time to time.

USE AN ILLUSTRATED SERMON—use people to "act" out the sermon (i.e. Jesus washing the feet of the disciples or the Lord's Supper). Have some background "props" to enhance the setting of the sermon (i.e. boat with fishing nets to emphasize the call for disciples to follow Christ). Dress the part of the Bible character you are presenting (i.e. Paul in chains/prison). The list is limitless. Allow the Holy Spirit to use your creativity.

USE APPROPRIATE ILLUSTRATIONS—an event from real life that can be applied to the lives of the congregation. (If you are using the story of someone in the congregation, be certain you obtain their permission to tell the story publicly.) A personal illustration can be quite effective; however, it must be presented in a manner that is not self serving (i.e. bragging about accomplishments, etc.).

USE HUMOR OCCASIONALLY—this will help to maintain the interest/attention of the congregation. The best humor is about yourself—something unusual or ridiculous that happened to you or that you did. Never make another person (who is in the congregation or known by the congregation) look foolish by your humor.

USE GRAPHICS AND MEDIA TECHNOLOGY (when available)—such as power point or a short video to give a visual presentation of the subject. Power Point is especially helpful in projecting Scriptures and the points of emphasis in the sermon. Many helpful tools are available free to those who have access to the internet and other aspects of the social media.

PROVIDE THE CONGREGATION WITH A PRINTED OUTLINE (if possible)—which will allow them to follow along with the sermon progression, as well as giving them a study tool for future reference. Some congregations use the Sunday morning sermon notes as a guide for home groups during the week. The degree of details contained in the notes is determined by the individual minister. Some chose a very detailed outline (as are noted in this volume); while others use a "fill-in-the-blanks" approach, so that the key points are written down by the congregation as the sermon is being preached. Still others provide only the main theme and sub-themes of the message.

HAVE THE CONGREGATION ASK QUESTIONS—at the end of the sermon, either verbally or in writing. This will not only clarify certain areas of truth for the questioner and congregation, but will also assist you in (1) understanding the concerns/interest of the people, and (2) developing a more easily comprehensible pattern for preaching.

BE YOURSELF! Remember, God has called you! You are unique and should not be embarrassed that you are not like someone else. God has placed you where you are for the completion of His purpose—both in and through you!

1 STORY TELLING—WITH SCRIPTURAL APPLICATION

People love stories, especially when they can personally "identify" with the details. Of course, our Lord was a master communicator. And, He very often told stories. Generally speaking, we refer to the stories in His teaching as parables. Many scholars suggest that there are 36 different parables in the Gospels.

A parable is a story that refers to something commonly understood by the audience to which the speaker will apply a truth that is not as easily understood. For example, during the time of Christ, the vast majority of that culture was supported by an agricultural lifestyle. Consequently, Jesus spoke of seeds, types of soil, harvest. He spoke of sheep and shepherds, of birds and flowers—common things that these people would know very well.

Usually, the intent of a parable is to emphasize one major truth. While more than one lesson may be derived from a parable, the preacher should be careful that he does not attempt to develop a "doctrine" from one portion of a parable. Doctrinal truth must be supported by the whole body of Scripture.

The most important aspect of this style of preaching is to be certain that the "story" (or parable) has a spiritual application that is confirmed by Scripture. It should not be assumed that "telling a story" requires any less spiritual and practical preparation than other styles of sermon presentation. The desired end result is always to lift up Christ Jesus.

The Old Testament is filled with narratives, as are the Gospels and book of Acts in the New Testament. However, from the book of Romans through Revelation there are no "stories." Consequently, the preacher who uses this method of preaching will often look to the Old Testament for the initial Scriptural reference point.

As an example, consider the story of Israel's defeat of Jericho—their first battle upon entering the Promised Land (Joshua 5:13-6:27). What lessons can be learned from this Biblical narrative and rightfully applied to our lives today?

FROM A FORTIFIED CITY TO A PILE OF ROCKS! (JOSHUA 5-6)

1. Obedience is required for victory.

2. Confirmation of God's plan for His people Israel.

3. Assurance for Joshua that God had chosen him to lead Israel.

4. Sin/evil must be completely destroyed.

Any one of these truths (and perhaps others) could be selected when using this story as the Scriptural "story" in a sermon. Again, the application must bring the hearers to a better understanding of the eternal plan of God as fully revealed in Christ Jesus.

Another Bible story—Gideon's defeat of the Midianites with 300 men (Judges 6-7). What truths are revealed in the Old Testament record?

300 MEN IN BATTLE WITH NO WEAPONS (JUDGES 6-7)

1. Disobedience always brings the judgment of God.

2. Self reliance (Pride) can never defeat the enemy.

3. Sincere questions do not anger God.

4. Faith is required in every situation of life.

5. Preparation for spiritual battle requires constant diligence.

6. Divine intervention does not rely on human methods.

People should remember the truth (application), not just the story!

There is a life time of preaching material to be found in God's Word. The man of God must not wait until the last minute to prepare the message. Fulfilling the sacred call must be his highest priority. Early in the history of the New Testament Church the apostles had to make a decision about their primary assignment: "we will continue to devote ourselves steadfastly to prayer and the ministry of the Word" (Acts 6:4 AMP).

THE FOLLOWING IS AN EXAMPLE OF A "STORY TELLING" OUTLINE:

TITLE: A LITTLE MAID'S QUIET TESTIMONY

TEXT: 2 Kings 5:2-3

THEME: Living out our faith under difficult circumstances will always provide opportunities to be a witness for Christ

INTRODUCTION:

These two verses contains everything we know about this "young girl." She was a "captive from Israel" and was serving as a "maid to Naaman's wife." The Old Testament account of Naaman's healing is well known. (Jesus referred to Naaman's healing in Luke 4:27.) He is described in Scripture as the "commander" (top general) of the Syrian armies, "a mighty warrior" for whom the King of Syria had "great admiration." But, "he suffered from leprosy" (a contagious skin disease, often spoken of in the Bible, and used as a "type" to indicate the harm/contamination of sin).

What is normally remembered about this story is that Elisha the prophet told him to "Go and wash in Jordan seven times" and how angrily Naaman reacted to the prophet's instruction. However, after he was willing to do as Elisha had instructed him he was totally cleansed of the leprosy.

But, we often overlook the person that God used to bring about this miracle—a little foreign maid who shared her faith and confidence in God's power to heal. She did not have a prominent position; as a captive, certainly no political influence. One could easily assume that her life had little value or meaning—but today, almost 3,000 years later, we are still talking about her influence.

Perhaps some here identify with her situation—feeling "trapped" in your circumstance, without any hope of relief. But do not despair—for God can/will use your life right where you are!

I. Position in life does not prevent expression of faith.

    A. God has chosen both rulers and servants; both wealthy and impoverished; both educated and uneducated; both men and women; both young and older to share the message of redemption in Christ.

    B. Each of us has opportunity to uniquely influence others in our sphere of associations .

        1. The message is not cultural, but it must be contextualized, not compromised by the influence of culture (Jesus used examples from agriculture—i.e. "seed/sower" —).

        2. Personal experience is irrefutable testimony Reference: Man born blind—(Read: John 9:24-25, 28-34).

        3. Family—always first priority.

    C. Life that has been changed (known to be different from previous lifestyle) speaks dramatically to every segment of society Reference: Woman at the well in Samaria—John 4:39.

    D. View your position as divine opportunity.

        1. To represent Him (2 Corinthians 5:20) .

        2. To invest in something larger than "self" desires.

II. Integrity of character provides door of opportunity for testimony.

    A. Influence is not determined by position

        1. Influence is based on "earned respect" (Consistency + Time = Respect).

        2. Person whose word can be trusted—honesty Jesus—*"Just say a simple, 'Yes, I will,' or 'No, I*

won't.' *Anything beyond this is from the evil one."*
(Matthew 5:37 NLT) (SEE; James 5:12)

B. Scriptural guidelines for "employees" *"Work willingly
at whatever you do, as though you were working for the
Lord rather than for people."* (Colossians 3:23 NLT)

    1. Don't be lazy—work consistently/diligently *"Lazy
people want much but get little, but those who
work hard will prosper."* (Proverbs 13:4 NLT)

    2. Don't be obstinate—make it difficult for employer
*"Servants...try to please them (employers) all
the time, not just when they are watching you."*
(Colossians 3:22 NLT)

    3. Don't be dishonest—with time or other things
*"Serve them sincerely because of your reverent fear
of the Lord."* (Colossians 3:22 NLT)

C. Developing relationships—knowing how to "get
along."

    1. Wisdom of words— *"Timely advice is lovely, like
golden apples in a silver basket."* (Proverbs 25:11
NLT)

        a. When to speak (appropriate time/place).

        b. What to speak (encouraging, constructive).

        c. How to speak (tactfully, kindly, etc.).

    2. Don't be a "know-it-all" *"Anyone who claims to
know all the answers doesn't really know very
much."* (1 Corinthians 8:2 NLT)

    3. Don't be the "champion of every cause."
*"Interfering in someone else's argument is as
foolish as yanking a dog's ears."* (Proverbs 26:17
NLT)

D. Don't "condemn" others by "flaunting" your "experience" *"If someone asks you about your Christian hope, always be ready to explain it. But do this in a gentle and respectful way."* (1 Peter 3:15-16 NLT)

    1. What we are is only by the grace of God.

    2. Reveal the joy of forgiveness, rather than the condemnation of judgment.

III. Ways of expressing your testimony.

A. By daily example of Christ-like life *"Be careful to live properly among your unbelieving neighbors. Then even if they accuse you of doing wrong, they will see your honorable behavior..."* (1 Peter 2:12 NLT)

    1. To "preach" without "practicing" is the worst form of "hypocrisy."

    2. Not everyone will show you respect as they are condemned by a godly life (John 3:18-20).

B. By "befriending" persons marginalized by society> Jesus was criticized—*"He's a friend of tax collectors and other sinners..."*(Matthew 11:19 NLT)

    1. Not avoiding them.

    2. Not speaking "down" (harshly) to them.

    3. Not "berating" them to others.

C. By assisting others in times of crisis.

    1. Helpful in meaningful ways (Reference: Good Samaritan—Luke 10:30-37).

    2. Words of comfort, assurance (especially, if you have had similar experience).

D. By serving without expectation of recognition.

    1. Personal initiative—not anticipated/required.

2. *"Let someone else praise you, not your own mouth..."* (Proverbs 27:2 NLT)

E. By maintaining a right attitude in adversity.

1. Criticism/abuse for your faith (John 15:18-19).

2. Expressing confidence in God's sovereign wisdom.

CONCLUSION:

God has "placed" us where we are for a diving purpose.

Each day we must be sensitive to doors of opportunity that He opens for us.

It may be just a few words,

a spontaneous act of kindness,

sharing a personal experience...

For someone your life will make a difference!!

2 TOPICAL—RELEVANT SUBJECT/SCRIPTURAL REFERENCES

The "topical" sermon is perhaps the most popular and frequently used. Simply, there is one major theme presented in the message, supported with various Scriptures from throughout the Word of God, which amplify and clarify this particular subject. This approach is especially valuable in presenting a series of messages (several consecutive) on one related theme. As an example:

Praying for the miracle (Acts 12:5, 12-17; James 5:17-18)

Preparing for the miracle (Exodus 12:3-11; 40-42)

Participating in the miracle (1 Corinthians 12:12-27; Colossians 3:17)

Proclaiming the miracle (Mark 15:18-20)

Perpetuating the miracle (Psalm 78:5-7; Matthew 28:18-20)

The Bible is a very practical book, giving instruction concerning many aspects of the daily life of a believer (i.e., relationships with others—family, friends, employees, even enemies; how to be a good steward of your finances; faith during difficult circumstances, etc.).

THE FOLLOWING IS AN EXAMPLE OF A TOPICAL SERMON:

(Notice the components of the outline)

TITLE: A THRONE OR A TOWEL?

TEXT: John 13:3-17

THEME: Being a servant to others is a Scriptural principle every believer should desire/seek to attain

INTRODUCTION:

The account of Jesus washing the disciples' feet is recorded only in the Gospel of John. The event takes place just a few hours before Christ is betrayed by Judas, when the disciples were gathered for the Passover meal. Not yet realizing the significance of this moment, the Twelve were still debating who would be the "greatest" in the Kingdom (Compare the time of Luke 22:24-30 with the text passage). In order to graphically illustrate the message He desired for them to learn, Jesus took the position of a low ranking household servant and washed their feet. This was a common courtesy offered to guests upon arrival at the home of a person with servants, as the roads were dusty and the shoes they wore were open-toed sandals. It was more than a symbolic act. Their feet were actually dirty!

There are several lessons that have great significance in this event:

1. This was private not public. That is, this was not done in open view for others to observe. There was

no "influence" or praise to be gained by washing a person's feet.

2. This was personal. It could only be done for one person at a time; this was not a "group" activity. In other words, it was an intentional act of servanthood toward that individual.

3. The distinction that Jesus made was that this was a "top-down" act, rather than the normal pattern of the lesser serving the greater. It was a dramatic departure from the norm by leaders in most cultures of the world. Such behavior would have been degrading, shameful, or totally unacceptable.

4. The lesson that Jesus was teaching His followers was that such a willingness to serve others included their peers; that is, their "equals." This too, was a novel concept for those who desired to have positions of prominence. So far as the Scriptural record is concerned, there are no later references to quarrels among the disciples concerning position.

I. Everyone is equal at the cross.

   A. Christianity does not automatically change role in life; it does change relationship.

      1. Paul to Philemon—concerning Onesimus ("useful").

         a. A runaway slave, who had robbed his master (Philemon 18).

         b. Converted under ministry of Paul in Rome (Philemon 10).

         c. Paul appeals for Philemon to take him

back/forgive wrongs (Philemon 17).

   d.   Accept him as a "brother." *"He is no longer like a slave to you, for he is a beloved brother...now he will mean much more to you, both as a man and as a brother in the Lord."* (Philemon 16 NLT)

  2. *"Slaves, obey your earthly masters with deep respect and fear. Serve them sincerely as you would serve Christ."* (Ephesians 6:5 NLT) *"Masters, treat your slaves in the same way. Don't threaten them; remember, you both have the same Master in heaven, and he has no favorites."* (Ephesians 6:9 NLT)

B. There are no distinctions in God's love. *"For you are all one in Christ Jesus."* (Galatians 3:28 NLT) (note distinctions of Galatians 3:26-29)

    Jew or Gentile (Religious or pagan).

    Slave or free (without or with personal rights).

    Male or female (more or less "status").

C. None "good enough" to deserve God's grace. None "too bad" to receive God's grace.

II. Being a servant is a direct assault on pride.

A. By "world's" standard—"Leader" is served by one of lesser importance or position.

  1. Peter initially refused to allow Christ to wash his feet (John 13:8).

  2. Jesus taught: *"Whoever wants to be a leader among you must be your servant, and whoever wants to be first among you must be the slave of everyone else."* (Mark 10:44-45 NLT)

3. Pride of being diminished in the opinion of others.

4. Pride of misunderstood motivation.

B. By "world's" standard—"Peers" must contend for themselves.

1. Disciples erroneously assumed their worth above peers.

2. Jesus taught: *"Since, I your Lord and Teacher, have washed your feet, you ought to wash each other's feet. I have given you an example to follow."* (John 13:14-15 NLT)

3. Pride of position of equality—not be a servant to equals.

4. Pride of improper motivation to be above others.

C. Pride must be "nailed to the cross" and the Christ like spirit of humility will lead us to be servants to others. *"The Son of Man came not to be served but to serve others..."* (Matthew 20:28 NLT)

III. Practical expressions of servanthood as followers of Christ.

A. Serving sincerely—(Latin word--without wax, signifying pure) *"Work willingly at whatever you do, as though you were working for the Lord rather than for people."* (Colossians 3:23 NLT) Not for man's recognition or approval--for God's glory.

B. Serving spontaneously—Parable of the "Good Samaritan" (Luke 10:30-37 NLT) He *"saw the man, he felt compassion for him..." "soothed his wounds... bandaged them...took him to an inn...paid the innkeeper..."*

C. Serving sensitively—*"Therefore, whenever we have the opportunity, we should do good to everyone— especially to those in the family of faith.*" (Galatians 6:10 NLT)

   1. Being led by the Spirit to be aware of "needs" of others.

   2. Even the smallest of deeds (*"even a cup of cold water to one of the least of my followers..."*) will be rewarded. (Matthew 10:42 NLT)

D. Serving sympathetically—"*Share each other's burdens, and in this way obey the law of Christ.*" (Galatians 6:2 NLT)

   1. In times of emergency/crisis.

   2. To allay fears, concerns of less mature in Christ.

E. Serving secretly—

   1. Public display of service negates eternal reward (Read: Matthew 6:1-18).

   2. Try serving without others (including the person served) knowing who the "servant" was.

F. Serving sacrificially—

   1. Paul recounts his many "sacrifices" (Read: 2 Corinthians 6:3-13).

   2. Service by Godly servants does not consider sacrifice (Read: Matthew 25:31-40 "When did we ever...").

G. Serving shamelessly—

   1. "*We live unto constant danger of death because we serve Jesus...*" (2 Corinthians 4:5-18 NLT)

   2. "*Our dedication to Christ makes us look like fools...*" (Read: 1 Corinthians 4:10-13 NLT)

CONCLUSION:

What are you reaching for? A throne or a towel?

3 TEXTUAL—SUBJECT CHOSEN FROM WORDS OF TEXT

A textual sermon can be easily identified as it takes the major theme and "sub-themes" directly from the Scripture. As an example in Paul's final letter to Timothy, the Apostle is encouraging the young pastor to endurance in his faith walk. He uses three examples to emphasize this message. They logically form the "major points" or "sub-themes" for a textual outline.

Determined Endurance (2 Timothy 2:1-6).

    I.   Devotion of a Soldier (verses 3-4).

    II. Discipline of an Athlete (verse 5).

    III. Determination of a Farmer (verse 6).

Another example could be taken from the words of our Lord as He is teaching about our attitude toward those who are considered to be our "enemies."

Loving your enemies (Luke 6:27-28).

    I.   Do good to those who hate You (verse 27).

    II. Bless those who curse you (verse 28).

    III. Pray for those who hurt you (verse 28).

NOTE: Jesus immediately made an application of how to show that you love your enemies (Read: Luke 6:29-30).

THE FOLLOWING IS AN EXAMPLE OF A TEXTUAL OUTLINE:

Since this is taken from The Beatitudes, one might also choose to make this a "series" of eight sermons, each message focusing on only one of the Beatitudes.

NOTE: Other Scriptures are used to emphasize, confirm the truth of the text passage. By citing various passages, several good things are accomplished: (1) evidence that this truth is taught throughout the Word; (2) provides references for further in depth study by members of the congregation; and (3) allows the pastor to have Scriptural illustrations to more clearly explain the message.

TITLE: EIGHT WAYS TO BE BLESSED

TEXT: Matthew 5:1-12

THEME: Blessings from God begin when man's spirit comes to a place of recognition and surrender to His redemptive plan for man's fulfillment in this life.

INTRODUCTION:

Matthew's Gospel account was written primarily to a Jewish audience. Considered as a natural "bridge" between the Old and New Testaments, this first Gospel emphasizes the teaching ministry of Christ. Matthew did not attempt to arrange the material in a chronological order, but rather wrote thematically. (Reference: The Parables of the Kingdom—Chapter 13 or the Prophetic Discourse—Chapters 24, 25) Scholars place this teaching—The Sermon on the Mount—after Christ had selected the 12 disciples, and during His Galilean ministry, the relatively short period of his popularity.

The Beatitudes, as this passage is often called, deals with the foundational principles for receiving/enjoying the blessings of God.

The word "Blessed"...happy, to be envied, and spiritually prosperous—with life-joy and satisfaction in God's favor, regardless of their outward conditions (Amplified), speaks to a quality of life that is both uncommon and impossible to achieve outside of the realm of the spirit. All of these promises of Christ seem like contradictions, for they are just the opposite of how the natural mind thinks.

I. Who do you think you are?

"Poor in spirit—rich in eternity."

A. Root word is "beggar": implies being at another's mercy, with no personal resources.

B. The despair of hopelessness *"Without Christ...without hope"* (Ephesians 2:12).

C. The truth about us all *"Once you were dead, doomed forever because of your many sins..."* *"We were born with an evil nature..."* (Ephesians 2:1-3)

D. Recognizing His worthiness *"Jesus came to take away our sins, for there is no sin in him."* (1 John 3:5 NLT) (Also 2 Corinthians 5:21; 1 Peter 3:18) *"And they sung a new song, saying, Thou art worthy to take the book, and to open the seals thereof: for thou wast slain, and hast redeemed us to by thy blood out of every kindred, and tongue, and people, and nation."* (Revelation 5:1-14—in heaven; KJV)

E. Foolishness of assuming self-determination.

   1. Don't "need" God—self-sufficient (Luke 12:16-21).

   2. Don't "want" God—self-gratification (Romans 1:21-22).

   3. Final accountability before God (Romans 14:12; 1 Peter 4:4-5).

II. You need to be sad! "Mourn—be comforted."

A. Own personal weakness.

   1. David plead with God over his sin (Psalm 51).

   2. Peter "wept" after denying Christ 3 times (Mark 14:66-72).

   3. Sin is not to be taken lightly.

B. Grieve over what grieves God.

   1. Rejection of His love by His creation (Jeremiah 2:13, 31-32).

2. Disobedience of His commandments (Matthew 23:37).

3. Injustice/suffering (Matthew 9:36).

III. Meekness is not weakness. "Meek—Inherit the Earth."

A. Implies "disciplined self control"—the opposite of self-will toward God and ill-will toward men.

B. Humility before God—accepting without resisting.

   1. Habakkuk did not understand God's methods but waited for His answer (Habakkuk 1-3).

   2. Paul's "thorn in the flesh" brought rejoicing because the power of Christ was resting on him (2 Corinthians 12:6-10).

   3. Moses was a "meek" man (Numbers 12:3) Did not defend himself against Aaron/Miriam.

C. Opposite of self-assertiveness.

   1. Christ was *"Meek and lowly of heart..."* (Matthew 11:29; 1 Peter 2:23)

   2. King David refused to kill King Saul (1 Samuel 24 and 26) or defend himself against Absalom (2 Samuel 15-19).

   3. Paul—*"Alexander ...did me much harm, but the Lord will judge him for what he has done."* (2 Timothy 4:14 NLT)

IV. How's your appetite? "Hunger and thirst for righteousness—be filled."

A. Basis for spiritual life.

   1. His presence (Exodus 33:14; Psalm 34:18; 145:18).

   2. The Word (Psalm 119:130).

   3. Communion with Christ (1 John 1:3; 2:28).

    4. Fellowship of the Spirit (John 14:17, 26).

  B. The desire for "righteousness"is both initial and
     continuous; progression from the desire to be forgiven
     by Christ to the desire to be conformed to His image.
     (2 Corinthians 3:18; 2 Peter 1:4)

The first four Beatitudes speak of the inner working of the
Spirit, while the second four identify the external evidences
of the Spirit's work.

V. Go easy—it could be you! "Merciful—be shown mercy."

  A. Mercy is a characteristic of God Himself (Psalm 103:17;
     Lamentations 3:22-23; Ephesians 2:4; Titus 3:5) Mercy—
     God not giving us what we deserve.

  B. Mercy is a principle of life for believers.

    1. Abraham—to his nephew Lot (Genesis 13).

    2. Joseph—to his brothers (Genesis 45 and 50).

    3. Moses—to Aaron and Miriam (Numbers 12).

    4. King David—to King Saul (1 Samuel 24).

    5. Jesus—to those who crucified Him (Luke 23:34).

  C. Mercy disallows personal "judgment" of others
     (Matthew 7:1-5).

    1. Does not imply condoning sin.

    2. Judging speaks of determining penalty for wrong
      doing (often harsh).

    3 Mercy does not define another's motivation (give
      "benefit-of-doubt").

  D. Mercy is an attitude that is reflected in kindness
     toward others who are different than we are or who
     disagree with us.

VI. Nothing to hide. "Pure in heart—see God."

A. Three components to walk with God.

　　1. Head knowledge—understanding of Word.

　　2. Hand labors—service to the Lord/His Church.

　　3. Heart relationship—purity before God/men.

B. External ceremony or works alone are inadequate.

　　1. God to Samuel—*"The Lord doesn't make decisions the way you do! People judge by the outward appearance, but the Lord looks at a person's thoughts and intentions."* (1 Samuel 16:7 NLT)

　　2. David's prayer—*"But you (God) desire honesty from the heart, so that you can teach me to be wise in my inmost being."* (Psalm 51:6 NLT)

C. A pure heart is void of guile (deceit, duplicity), hypocrisy.

　　1. Jesus condemned the religious leaders—not for their works, but for their hypocrisy (Read: Matthew 23).

　　2. Shame, disgrace come to cause of Christ by negative influence of "impure hearts."

D. A pure heart has nothing to hide!

　　1. What you say will always be the same! (Not have to remember what you said—if it is truth.)

　　2. What you do will be without shame!

VII. Agreeing to a cease fire is not peace. "Peacemakers—Children of God."

A. *"Makers and maintainers of peace."* (Amplified)

B. No one is at peace with the world who is not at peace with himself!

C. The initiative must be with the Child of God. *"Do*

your part to live in peace with everyone, as much as possible." (Romans 12:1 NLT)

D. Peace is more than the absence of conflict (hostility).

    1. Home (1 Peter 3:1-7; Ephesians 5:21-6:4).

    2. House of God (Ephesians 4:1-4; 2 Corinthians 13:11).

E. Maintaining peace requires constant diligence and willingness to make adjustments/changes *"Only by pride cometh contention..."* (Proverbs 13:10 NLT)

VIII. You know you are on the right road. "Persecuted for righteiousness—Kingdom of Heaven."

A. This is "undeserved" persecution.

    1. "For righteousness sake..."

    2. "Speak against you falsely..." (for following Christ)

B. Persecution is a "blessing in disguise" to believers.

    1. Recognize dependence on Christ.

    2. Kept in place of humility.

    3. Gain in faith/grow in spiritual maturity.

C. Storing up eternal reward! *"But if we are to share in his glory, we must also share in his suffering. Yet what we suffer now is nothing compared to the glory he will give us later."* (Romans 8:17-18 NLT) *"Instead, be very glad—because the trials will make you partners with Christ in his suffering, and afterward you will have the wonderful joy of sharing his glory..."* (1 Peter 4:12-19 NLT)

PRACTICAL LESSONS:

1. Very obvious omission: Jesus did not mention earthly

"possessions" in this list of ways to be happy and fulfilled in this life.

2. Man's fulfillment must begin with the spiritual life, then will proceed to the mind and physical body.

3. If your "attitude" toward God is right, it will naturally follow that it is right toward others.

4. Man's desire must be to have a right relationship with God—then, and only then, will the fullness of His blessings overflow.

4 EXPOSITORY—THEME CHOSEN FROM EXTENDED PASSAGE

For many scholars and Bible teachers, the "expository" sermon is the most effective style of preaching, especially for the pastor. In effect, this will assure that the "whole counsel of God" is presented in a systematic manner. By definition, the expository sermon will take an extended passage, select the overall theme from those verses and find the "sub-themes" within the passage. Unlike the topical sermon, which includes Scripture verses from various locations other than the text, this sermon will almost exclusively confine itself to the one segment of Scripture being expounded. The key to an effective expository sermon is to first of all to identify the one main theme and carefully focus on that one thought. In most passages more than one theme can be located quite easily. It is a discipline for the preacher to refrain from jumping from subject to subject in a single sermon!

To present the Word "verse by verse" is a good teaching method where there is opportunity for interaction (i.e. small home group discussions, Sunday School classes, etc.). However, in a regular church service, where time is often limited and the level of spiritual understanding and maturity of the audience may vary significantly, too much information without focusing on a specific subject/theme can be overwhelming or confusing to some who are less knowledgeable of the Word.

THE FOLLOWING IS AN EXAMPLE OF AN EXPOSITORY SERMON OUTLINE:

As you review the outline below, note the following:

1. There is one major theme—God's Deliverance in difficult circumstances.

2. The six sub themes are taken directly from the text passage, and progressively lead us to the conclusion that God will intervene in our behalf.

3. The application explains and applies the Biblical passage to contemporary life—God will be our deliverer during the intense struggles that we encounter.

TITLE: THE VALLEY OF BLESSING

TEXT: 2 Chronicles 20:1-30

THEME: Even in the difficult times of life, God will reveal Himself and bring deliverance

INTRODUCTION:

Jehoshaphat, fourth King of Judah, had become mighty, and was highly respected by the kings and nations around him (2 Chronicles 18:1). However, a group of three nations joined in an alliance against him. When Jehoshaphat heard of this approaching vast army, he immediately called all the people of Judah to a solemn fast. Ultimately God gave them a great victory, without even having to engage in battle. This is a powerful record of God's intervention into the lives of His people, when they face danger (trials). As a memorial to this great, unusual victory, they named the place the valley of blessing.

I. Proclamation (verses 5-9)

> *"You alone are God..."*
>
> *"You are ruler of all the kingdoms of this earth..."*
>
> *"You are powerful and mighty, no one can stand against you..."*

II. Petition (verses 10-12)

> *"We are powerless against this mighty army..."*
>
> *"We do not know what to do..."*
>
> *"We are looking to you for help..."*

III. Promise (verses 13-17)

> *"Do not be afraid..."*
>
> *"Do not be discouraged..."*
>
> *"The battle is not yours, but God's!"*
>
> *"Stand still and watch the Lord's victory!"*
>
> *"The Lord is with you..."*

IV. Praise (verses 20-23)

> *"Singers to walk ahead of the army..."*
>
> (Almost 20 km to Jerusalem—faith required)
>
> *"Singing to the Lord..."*
>
> *"Praising him for his holy splendor..."*
>
> *"Give thanks unto the Lord; His faithful love endures forever!"*

V. Plunder (verses 24-26)

> *"Vast amounts of equipment, clothing, and other valuables..."*
>
> *"Took them three days to collect it all..."*
>
> (Such material blessings were not the primary

concern—God added these because of their faith/ obedience.)

VI. Peace (verses 27-31)

"Marched into Jerusalem full of joy..."

"Marched into Jerusalem to music..."

"Proceeded to the Temple..."

"Surrounding nations heard—the fear of the Lord came on them..."

"Kingdom was at peace, for God had given them rest on every side..."

THE VALLEY OF BLESSING

A. Valley often symbolized as "trial" or "test" in Scripture

Psalm 23:4 *"the dark valley of death," "I will not be afraid, for you are close beside me."*

Psalm 84:6 *"Valley of Weeping" "It will become a place of refreshing springs, where pools of blessing collect after the rains!"*

Joshua 7:24-26; Hosea 2:15 *"Valley of Trouble" "I will transform the Valley of Trouble into a gateway of hope."*

1. If there are mountains...there must also be valleys. Mountains are for blessing; valleys are for growing.

2. No miracle without a crisis.

3. Valleys increase dependence on the Lord.

   a. To change the impossible circumstance.

   b. To provide grace during/through the circumstance.

4. Valleys show the might/power of God to do the humanly impossible (2 Chronicles 16:7; Psalm 62:11;

Psalm 89:10, 13; Psalm 106:8).

B. Battle came at a time of spiritual renewal (2 Chronicles 19).

C. Undeserved attack from enemy (verse 10).

    1. Satanic attacks come without provocation.

        a. Example of Job (Job 1 and 2).

        b. Persecution of believers in NT Church—Theme in 1 Peter is "Victory in Suffering" (Paul/Peter warn believers of persecution).

        c. Spiritual war from forces of "darkness" (2 Corinthians 10:3-5; Ephesians 6:10-18; 2 Corinthians 12:7-10).

    2. Satan delights in "challenging" faith (Genesis 3:4, 5; Job 1 and 2; Tempted Christ—Matthew 4:1-11).

D. Pattern of faith—Faith is developed in adversity.

    1. Called for a fast among all the people.

    2. Waited on the Lord.

    3. Heard the Word of the Lord (prophet).

    4. Bowed and worshipped God.

    5. Stood and praised the Lord.

E. Sounds like a paradox—Blessing in a Valley.

    1. *"All things work together for good/God's purpose…"* (Romans 8:28).

    2. God uses difficulties to strengthen our faith (James 1:2-4).

    3. In valley, learn our weaknesses.

    4. In valley, discover new depth of relationship with God (Psalms 42:5-11; 43:5; 2 Corinthians 12:9).

5. Become more conformed to HIS image
   (2 Corinthians 4:16-18).

6. Able to encourage/assist others in similar
   circumstances (2 Corinthians 1:3-6).

CONCLUSION:

When you have safely crossed to the other side of the valley, you will look back and see all that God has done. Your valley has become a great blessing!

The Walk of Faith will never become the walk of sight.

Hold firmly to the Master's hand—He has already travelled this way before.

EIGHT

PREPARING THE SERMON

N ow, it is time to develop the sermon outline. Remember, this is only a tool to assist you! It may be possible to cut down a large tree with a knife, but a sharp ax will do the job much more quickly.

Your preaching skills will continue to improve as you allow the Holy Spirit to anoint your mind. Since the Holy Spirit is God, He can guide your thoughts through prayer, study, and sermon preparation. And, He also knows the future.

"Advance" preparation for pulpit ministry does not negate the work of the Holy Spirit in directing your thinking, nor will it diminish the anointing on the presentation.

Before you even begin seeking the Lord for a message, He is already aware of who will be in the congregation on that occasion and what their spiritual needs are!

The purpose of the outline is not to restrict or confine; rather, it is simply a guide that will help you stay on course. Like a highway it will bring you in the direction you want to go. If you abandon the highway for a shortcut, you may go in the wrong direction and ultimately find yourself where you did not plan to be. The more you prepare sermon outlines, the more comfortable you begin to feel in using it to assist you in communicating your thoughts. Although most do not, some preachers prepare a full manuscript (write out the sermon word for word), learn the content as the Lord has given it to them, and then only refer to it at specific times when in the pulpit. The point is that each individual must find what is comfortable for them. But, as we shall see, there is tremendous value in having sermon material organized and written.

> The anointing of the Holy Spirit is not measured by volume in the voice of the preacher, nor by the rapidity with which he speaks; rather by the content of the message in exalting Christ and bringing glory to God.

ORGANIZE YOUR THOUGHTS—THEME, SUBTHEMES, ETC.

Once you have been directed by the Holy Spirit to a particular passage of Scripture, it is important to begin to organize your thoughts. What is the theme (subject) of the message? What is the style of this particular sermon (i.e. topical, textual, expository)? What subthemes do I wish to present? Are they in the text passage or do I search for other Scriptures to illuminate these truths? Does the outline logically progress from one point to the next in a manner that will build to the conclusion? These are not difficult questions, yet, if you discipline yourself to clearly set forth what you want to say, your preaching will be powerful and effective.

> Effective pulpit ministry does not make a simple truth confusing...
>
> Effective pulpit ministry will make the difficult truth easy to understand...
>
> Great preachers will so enlighten the hearers that they will wonder why they did not comprehend this Biblical truth earlier!

By having his thoughts well organized....

1. The preacher will avoid unnecessary repetition of the same material in his sermon.

2. The preacher will reduce the repeated use of words/phrases that do not specifically contribute to the content of the message (i.e. "Can somebody say Amen", etc.).

3. The preacher will progress from the introduction to

the conclusion of the message in a systematic manner
that can easily be remembered by the congregation.

WRITE IT DOWN!

This guide for preparing your sermon outline is simple, yet will
allow you to have a logical pattern to follow as you begin to
prayerfully develop each message.

❶ Title: The subject of the message should be stated in a very
few words, rather than a complete sentence. It should capture the
imagination of the audience so they will be eager to hear the content of the sermon.

❷ Scripture passage (Bible reference—book, chapter, verses)

❸ Objective of the message: This will be a short statement (usually one descriptive sentence) explaining the truth that will be
emphasized. Often called the "propositional" statement, as it pro-
poses the conclusion that will be reached by the message.

❹ Introduction: Each will be introduction will be unique, vary-
ing from message to message. Some ideas that may be included
are:

- Relate the context of the passage.
- Tell the Bible story or identify the major characters in
  the text passage.
- Develop a "parable" (hypothetical story).
- Use an illustration from current events that assist in
  transitioning to the "body" of the sermon.
- Use media technology, showing a short video or
  testimony to enhance the subject of the message.

❺ Body of the sermon—Main divisions or subthemes: Up to this point, you have been telling the congregation what you are going to tell them. Now, in the "body" of the sermon you explain the Biblical truth by amplifying in greater detail each aspect of this truth. Again, these "sub themes" (divisions or points) should flow in a logical manner—each building on the previous sub theme and all moving forward toward the desired conclusion. The body of the message should be very carefully and prayerfully considered. The preacher must not jump back and forth between ideas, either by needless repetition of what has already been presented or injecting thoughts that will be contained in a later part of the message. Remember, the outline is to prevent the speaker from adding unrelated material that will leave the audience confused or, at least, uncertain of the intended focus of the sermon.

⑥ Summarize (briefly) the purpose: This should be a very brief— no more than two or three sentences—summary of the message, with careful emphasis on the original theme. This will neatly tie together the several subthemes for the congregation. Now, they have the "whole package" to take with them to their homes for further study, prayer, and meditation.

There are basically two kinds of altar invitations (call to a public response to the message...

One that requires *immediate action.* Included in this would be the call for repentance and salvation, prayer for the sick, seeking to be filled with the Holy Spirit, deliverance from sinful habits, and such like.

The other requires a *lifelong commitment.* Included in this invitation would be the call to obey the call of God for service, developing loving family relationships with spouse and children, being a good steward of financial resources, and such like.

It is always important to ask the congregation for a public response to the message. If they leave the church without personally waiting in the presence of God, very soon other activities will demand their attention and the conviction of the Holy Spirit will dissipate.

7 Conclusion: You have been telling the congregation what they should do; now, you must explain how they are to do it. This is the application. You have presented what the Word says, but for the message to be truly meaningful, believers must understand the action required to assimilate the Word into their daily living.

8 Invitation (salvation, baptism, healing, etc.): The "invitation" should always be prayerfully planned in coordination with the message. Of course, the Holy Spirit will direct you. On occasion He will guide the spiritual leader through a supernatural manifestation of one of the Gifts of the Spirit. This may not have been included in your planning. However, just as the Spirit has anointed your planning, preparation, and the presentation, He will also anoint the altar invitation.

NINE

KEEP A RECORD OF YOUR PREACHING

BY SUBJECT MATTER

If you serve as a pastor…

❶ It is important to know what you have preached, so that you do not repeat the same message with the same text within a brief period of time.

❷ It is important to know what you have preached, so that you will not become a *one dimensional* pastor, preaching repeatedly on the same subject (i.e. tithing, water baptism, second coming of Christ, etc.) to the exclusion of other significant Biblical truths. Believers should be growing in their faith walk and to do so they must be "fed" a balanced diet from the entire Word of God.

❸ It is important to know what you have preached for your own personal development and growth as a minister of the Gospel. The man of God must never become complacent or "satisfied" with his own level of Scriptural understanding. The Holy Spirit will reveal new insights into the Word as you study and pray!

BY DATE, LOCATION, AND OCCASION (SUNDAY MORNING, ETC.)

For years I kept a notebook listing information relating to each message. Today, if you have access to a computer, it is quite easy to regularly log in the information/data. As an example: you may wish to consider the simple form noted below or develop a form that will best suit your needs.

RECORD OF MINISTRY

Date: _____

Message subject/title: _____

Location: _____

Occasion:_____

Attendance: _____

Evaluation of service: (number saved, filled with Spirit, healed) ____

_____

Personal comments: _____

_____

Also, you may find it helpful to keep a similar list for:

- Water baptisms.

- Marriage ceremonies.

- Baby dedications.

- Funeral services.

- Other special occasions.

MAINTAIN THE NOTES FOR FUTURE REFERENCE

It is important to know what you preached for future reference. That is, you may desire to review the previous study/research of Scripture on a given subject. As you build your library of sermon outlines, they will assist you in preparing for future ministry. For example, the message of salvation by faith in Christ is foundational to all Christianity. Consequently, as the Spirit directs, you will frequently challenge sinners to accept Jesus. Even though the subject may be the same, the message itself will be different. However, you have already compiled various Scriptural references in your file of notes. By referring to these outlines/notes you may find a significant amount of information that can be integrated into another sermon.

How extensive should your sermon notes/outlines be? That, of course, is determined by your personal preference. As a general guide, you should write down enough so that when you review the notes again, you will remember what you said in that sermon a few weeks or months earlier!

If you have access to a computer or other technical device, you will find it extremely helpful to have the outlines/notes in a "sermon file." The information can be quickly located and easily accessed if you file it by subject matter (i.e., Salvation, Second Coming, Practical Christian Living, Baptism in the Holy Spirit, Divine Healing, etc.).

TEN

PREACHING—THE PRIVILEGE OF A LIFETIME!

*H*ave you ever wondered why God called you? Have you ever thought that there are so many others who have greater ability or qualifications than I do? Did you ever consider that out of more than seven billion people who now live on this earth that God chose you as His ambassador? I have been blessed and privileged to be one of His "spokespersons" for more than half a century. Even after all these years, I am still amazed (and thankful) that God has so favored my life.

Never, ever conclude that yours is a life of overwhelming burden and persistent difficulties. The ministry is not simply a duty that one must fulfill for fear of the consequences. Yes, there are challenges and crisis times that cause us to run to our Father in desperation. But, in those deep struggles just allow your mind to meditate on what Jesus did for us through His substitutionary death for our sins.

> *"For our present troubles are small and won't last very long. Yet they produce for us a glory that vastly outweighs them and will last forever! So we don't look at the troubles we can see now; rather we fix our gaze on things that cannot be seen. For the things we see now will soon be gone, but the things we cannot see will last forever."*
> (2 Corinthians 4:7-18 NLT)

It is the greatest privilege in the world to be one of His followers. And, to have the peaceful assurance of eternal salvation is *"joy unspeakable and full of glory"* (1 Peter 1:8). Then, as one of His chosen disciples in this generation, the expressions of our love for the Master through submissive service cannot be equaled by any earthly pleasure or reward.

"...let us run with endurance the race that God has set before us. We do this by keeping our eyes on Jesus, the originator and perfecter of our faith."
(Hebrews 12:2 NLT)

Will you allow the Spirit to confirm or re-affirm God's special call on your life in this moment? Wait in His presence—as you have done on many previous occasions. Hear that *"still, small voice"* (1 Kings 19:12) offering words of assurance and direction. You will not see, know, or ever fully understand all that God has in your future. Just trust Him. It will well be worth the journey of faithful obedience to that *"heavenly vision"*(Acts 26:19).

Preacher, lift up the Cross of Jesus Christ!

Preach the Word!

Be faithful to His call!

Jesus is building His Church—just as He promised!

Our Lord will return—very soon!

MY PERSONAL CALL:

MY PERSONAL COMMITMENT:

OTHER TITLES BY H. MAURICE LEDNICKY

KINGDOM LIVING

THE DNA OF FAITH:
BALANCING YOUR FAITH WITH THE SOVEREIGNTY OF GOD

FADED GLORY:
THE CHURCH IN A CULTURE CRISIS

THE SCRIPTURES APPLIED, VOLUMES I, II, AND III

Books can be ordered directly from:
www.lednickybooks.com
or
Lifestyle Ministries
1322 N Fenchurch Lane
Springfield, MO 65802
U.S.A.